09
10

Living with a
Pomeranian

Edited by Averil Cawthera

BARRON'S

THE QUESTION OF GENDER
The pronoun "he" is used throughout this book instead of the rather impersonal "it," but no gender bias is intended at all.

ACKNOWLEDGMENTS
The publisher would like to thank the following for help with photography: Mary Larrassey (Warleggan), Susan Steel (Sullews), Bill and Jean Stone (Billijees), and Patricia Phillips (Playalong).

First edition for the United States and Canada published 2003 by Barron's Educational Series, Inc.

© 2003 Ringpress Books

All inquiries should be addressed to:
Barron's Educational Series, Inc.
250 Wireless Boulevard
Hauppauge, New York 11788
http://www.barronseduc.com

International Standard Book Number 0-7641-5669-1

Library of Congress Catalog Card Number 2002117159

Printed in Singapore
9 8 7 6 5 4 3 2 1

CONTENTS

CHAPTER ONE

INTRODUCING THE POMERANIAN

With his glamorous, luxurious coat, and his alert, foxy face, the Pomeranian is everything you could wish for from a dog and more – intelligent, spirited, affectionate, and fun. This is a Toy breed that loves attention, but that also has quite an independent streak.

Playful, plucky, and exceptionally loving, the Pomeranian is a dog that belies his tiny size. This is not a breed that is content to be pampered on a lap all day. Although he enjoys cuddles with his owner, he also likes to be doing. This aspect of the Pom's character is very strong, and is a vestige from the days when he was a working dog – yes, a working dog!

SPITZ ANCESTRY

At first glance, it is hard to imagine how the tiny Pomeranian, weighing just 4 to 5 pounds (1.8–2.2 kg), is related to the large, tough spitz breeds of Iceland and Lapland. But if you compare the Pom to other spitz dogs, such as

the Alaskan Malamute or Samoyed, the similarity is remarkable, and you will see that the Pom is spitz-like in everything but size.

Spitz breeds include the Akita, Alaskan Malamute, Chow Chow, Norwegian Elkhound, Finnish Spitz, Keeshond, Samoyed, and Schipperke. All spitz types share the following common characteristics:

- Tail that is carried over the back (except the Schipperke)
- Erect, prick ears (essential for hearing approaching wolves or other predators of the flock that the breed was expected to protect)
- Thick, dense, double, waterproof coat to protect against harsh weather conditions.

Spitz types have an ancient ancestry, dating back 10,000 years. They were used for sledding, hunting, and herding in the harsh Nordic climate, and today are still known to have these strong instincts.

SPITZ BREEDS

Despite the differences in size, there is a distinct look to a spitz breed.

The Pomeranian: dainty and compact.

The Samoyed (left): medium-sized, strong and active.

The Akita (right): a large, powerful, dog.

POMERANIA POM

From northern Europe, the spitz breeds made their way around the continent. It was in Germany that the Pom flourished, taking its name from Pomerania, the northeast region of Germany that borders the Baltics. The breed was developed in this area, and was probably bred smaller, although the dogs were still many times larger than the Pom we know and love today. Early dogs weighed in the region of 50 pounds – ten times that of the modern breed!

Pomerania (meaning "of the sea") was a thriving sea-trading area, and this resulted in the spitz breeds also traveling south. Several jars and jugs dating from as early as 200 B.C. have been unearthed in Greece, depicting spitz-like companion dogs, and they are also featured in pharaohs' tombs in ancient Egypt.

Eastward, there is also evidence of Pom-like dogs. In *Voyage of Discovery Around the World*, the author, George Vancouver, describes how, in an Indian village in 1792, he chanced upon several dogs "resembling those from Pomerania, although somewhat larger." Interestingly, the dogs were prized for their coats – not on themselves but on their owners! The dogs were shaved, and their coats were made into blankets and clothing for the village folk.

BRITISH BIRTH

It is likely that Queen Charlotte, wife of King George III, knew of the dogs from Pomerania because she spent her childhood in the bordering region of Mecklenburg. A devoted dog lover, Charlotte brought the breed to the U.K. in

Queen Victoria became a great fan of the breed.

1767, after her husband became king in 1760. Two dogs, Phoebe and Mercury, accompanied her to Britain, and were kept in Kew, London. Fortunately for breed historians, the artist Thomas Gainsborough also lived in Kew, and included the dogs in several of his paintings.

Royalty led the fashions of the day, and the Pomeranian soon became popular with the aristocracy. At the time, the Pom weighed in the region of 30 to 35 pounds (13.6–15.8 kg). However, the occasional dwarf was born that was about a third of the size of his siblings. Weighing 10 to 12 pounds (4.5–5.4 kg) in adulthood, these "sports," as they were known, were very popular, and breeding programs were initiated to produce similar-sized Poms.

ROYAL APPROVAL

In the first Kennel Club Stud Book (1862–1873), there are several Pomeranians listed, including Alba, Blanco, Carlo, and Charlie. Poms were certainly around before this date, though.

The black Pom makes a striking exhibit in the show ring.

A "Pomeranian Fox Dog" was entered in the Foreign Dogs Non-Sporting category at a show in Birmingham, West Midlands, in 1859. Another, called Jack, was shown in London in 1862, and was offered for sale by his owner for ten guineas (ten pounds and ten shillings).

However, it was Queen Victoria, an avid dog fancier besotted with the Pomeranian, who had the greatest impact on the breed.

In 1888, on a royal visit to Florence, Italy, she acquired several Pomeranians, including a red sable, whom she named Marco. He was tiny for the time (12 lb/5.4 kg), and drew great interest at shows. It was Marco's influence that popularized the small Pom, and, during Queen Victoria's reign, breeders were consistently producing smaller dogs.

The breed received official Kennel Club recognition in 1870 as the Spitzdog, and the Pomeranian Club was formed in 1891.

In the early days of the breed, there were two size categories: over 8 pounds (3.6 kg) and under 8 pounds. Because of the fashion for small dogs, there were very few entries for the heavier variety, and, as a result, the weight categories were changed in 1894. The new categories included a Toy grouping for dogs weighing below 7 pounds.

A keen exhibitor, Queen Victoria entered her Poms at many shows. It was customary at the time for classes to be split into color varieties, so when the Queen wanted to exhibit a color not usually found in the U.K., she was given her own separate class!

In 1891, just before the breed standard was published (see Chapter Nine), Queen Victoria exhibited Marco (a red sable with almost white markings), Gina (a 7.5 lb/3.4 kg) white dog with lemon tinges), Lenda (a buff-colored dog with a white blaze on her face), and Fluffy (the product of a Marco-Lenda mating – who, like her mother, was buff-colored). Today, Marco, Gina, and Lenda would be considered mismarked, because of their white/lemon coloring.

Victoria's love of the breed stayed with her until her dying day. As the monarch lay on her deathbed in 1901, she was reported to have had Turi, her favorite Pom, by her side. The devoted pet stayed with his mistress until she died.

AMERICAN STARS

Fortunately, the breed continued to grow in popularity after Queen Victoria's death, and the British export of Poms to America expanded the gene pool.

The first Pomeranian to be registered by the American Kennel Club (AKC) was Dick, in 1888. Twelve years later, in 1900, the breed received official recognition, and the American Pomeranian Club was formed (founded by a Mrs. Smith and a Mrs. Williamson). The club was recognized by the AKC in 1909, and, in 1911, held its first specialty show in New York – which has now become an annual event.

FAMOUS OWNERS

Queen Victoria
Sir Isaac Newton
Michaelangelo
David Hasselhoff
Ozzy and Sharon Osbourne

COLORS

By the 1890s, there was a range of Pom coat colors, including white, beaver (a gray-brown color), black, blue, cream, parti-color (patches of white and a color), and shaded sable.

White and cream were initially prevalent, but from the post-war period onward, these pale coats diminished in popularity, and the foxy orange color became dominant – to such an extent that the other coat colors were neglected (almost to the point of disappearing entirely).

Concerted efforts by breeders over the last two decades have revived the range of colors, with red, orange, cream, sable, brown, blue, black and tan, brindle, and black being seen in the show ring.

See also page 100 for color descriptions.

RISE, FALL, RISE

By the turn of the 20th century, the Pomeranian was in huge demand as a pet and show dog, and breeders were churning out large numbers of puppies. Since they were commanding prices of up to £250, it is easy to see where the saying "There's money in Poms" came from!

The Pom's small size proved to be a saving grace during the war years.

With such large numbers of dogs being produced, and with little regard given to choosing quality stock from which to breed, the Pomeranian began to deteriorate (for example, heads became more rounded, rather than foxy). Fortunately, supply soon outstripped demand, and the breeding fervor came to an end – just in time to save the breed.

In 1915, the British Kennel Club declared that all weights of Pomeranian should be shown together (there were still two weight categories at this time). Fans of the heavier Pom were encouraged to register the dogs as "Spitz," but that breed never took off. The fashion for tiny Poms continued – on both sides of the Atlantic – and exhibits in the show ring became increasingly smaller, until they reached today's weight of around 4 to 5 pounds (1.8–2.2 kg).

Many breeds suffered a great deal during the two World Wars, but the Pom's size saved him. Unlike larger dogs that owners struggled to feed, it was not too difficult to scrape together a meal for a tiny Pom. Although numbers did fall, and shows were few and far between, there was not a significant decline in the breed.

Post war, however, the Pekingese found favor, followed by the Yorkshire Terrier, and the Pomeranian was ousted in the Toy dog popularity contest.

THE BREED TODAY

Over the last 20 years, however, the Pom has made a steady comeback – particularly in America, where the breed is hugely popular.

In the United States, the Pom is the sixth most popular breed, according to AKC statistics, with 20,080 dogs registered in 2001. This compares

Bright, alert, and affectionate, the Pom makes a superb companion.

with just 693 for British Kennel Club figures for the same year. In fact, in ten years, Pom numbers have nearly halved in the U.K. Pom registrations have fallen slightly in the United States too, but, since a similar dip is reflected in most other breeds, this can be attributed to the decrease in purebred dog ownership, rather than to a specific loss of interest in the Pom.

The decrease in the U.K. is likely to be due to supply – with such small litters (an average of two puppies and many singletons), and a 50 percent mortality rate among puppies, that doesn't leave the breeder with many dogs to sell! However, with the Pom being so immensely popular in the United States, it could be just a matter of time before the trend toward owning this glamorous ball of fluff catches hold in the U.K. too.

In both the U.K. and the United States, the Pomeranian is a popular show dog, and a much-loved family pet. But his skills do not stop there. Underneath the glamorous coat lies an active dog that enjoys training and working. This aspect of the breed is put to good use in America, where Pomeranians are trained in competitive Obedience, Agility, Flyball, herding, and carting (see Chapter Seven).

But it is as a companion dog that the Pomeranian really excels. The breed is acutely sensitive to the moods of his owner, and adjusts his behaviour accordingly. When a cuddle is needed, he's there! If you need cheering up, he'll try his best to make you laugh. The Pom is all things to all people – a lot of dog condensed in a tiny body!

CHAPTER TWO

CHOOSING A POM

S urely there can be no prettier breed than the Pom! Tiny and delicate, with a luxurious coat and an irresistible, foxy face, the Pomeranian is a charming dog that can melt the hardest of hearts. Do not be won over by looks alone, however. Although he is small, the Pom's demands are great – and he requires a certain type of home in which to thrive. Ask yourself the following questions – and be honest in your answers!

Can your children be trusted?

Pomeranians are not suitable pets for a family with young children. Although they love kids, Poms do not take kindly to rough handling and can be seriously injured by children who are not old enough to know better (see page 27). Each breeder has his or her own policy.

Children under five are out of the question with most breeders; some will sell to a family with well-behaved seven- or eight-year-olds, but some will rule out any family where the kids are under the age of ten.

Are your work commitments compatible with having a dog?

Being a Toy dog, the Pomeranian needs human company. Being left alone from 9 a.m. to 5 p.m. is no life for this breed (or, indeed, any dog), and he will be terribly unhappy if neglected in this way. Four hours is the maximum time he should be left – but the ideal home is one where there is somebody in the house all day.

Can you cope with the grooming?

Although he is tiny, grooming the Pom's thick, fluffy coat is a time-consuming business, and takes about three hours. This should be done once a week (in addition to a daily brushing) without fail. Will you be able to commit to this intensive routine for the next 15 or so years?

Clipping the coat, as you can do with other long-coated breeds, such as the Old English

The Pom may be a tiny Toy dog, but the responsibilities of ownership are the same as they are for a large breed.

Sheepdog, is not an option. You could choose to have the coat professionally groomed, but, in addition to these professional jobs, you still need to brush the coat regularly to keep it free from mats (see page 55).

Do you have the time to commit to a Toy dog?

As well as the regular grooming needed, you must be able to spend regular, quality time with your dog. He will need daily exercise, regular training and play sessions, and lots and lots of cuddle time! Sleeping in late will also be a thing of the past – the dog will need to go out to relieve himself first thing in the morning.

Can you afford a Pom?

Their feeding bills may be lower than those of most other breeds, but you still have all the equipment to buy (see page 23), kenneling/dog-sitting costs when you go on vacation, professional grooming, and, most significantly, veterinary fees. If you have not had a dog before, or not for some time, do not underestimate how much veterinary treatment costs – even for a small dog.

Are you fit and healthy?

Some dogs end up in rescue because their owners can no longer physically cope. Arthritic hands can make grooming impossible, and some people are unable to bend down to lift up their dogs. Plus, although the Pom does not require a lot of exercise, he should be taken out regularly to be mentally stimulated. You may be healthy now, but will this still be the case in 15 years?

FINDING A POM

If you are certain the Pom is the only breed for you, and that you can care for all his needs, then the next step is to find your perfect puppy.

You should buy only from a reputable breeder. He or she will be a specialist in the breed, should offer after-sales advice and support, and should take the puppy back if your circumstances change in a few years' time. By buying from such a breeder, you will also be able to assess the mother's conformation and temperament.

So, how do you find a reputable breeder? The first step is to contact your national kennel club for details about local Pomeranian breed clubs. You should call and inquire about reputable breeders with litters available. Be warned: You may have to wait some time for a litter to become available.

Pom puppies are enchanting, and almost impossible to resist.

Fine breeding

Once you locate a recommended breeder, have a long talk about their dogs, what you want from a dog, your lifestyle, and so on. Ask the following questions:

- How long has the breeder been involved in the breed? (The longer, the better.)
- How long has he/she been involved in breeding?
- How many litters does he/she produce each year? (Be wary of the prolific breeder.)
- Do they breed any other dogs? (Avoid those who breed many different dogs – those who specialize in one or two breeds are preferable.)
- Why do they breed? (For money, glory, or for the good of the breed?)
- Find out about the parents – why were they chosen? Can the mother be seen? Who is the sire? (Never view a litter unless the mother of the puppies is present.)
- Are there any health problems in the breeder's line?
- Where will the puppies be raised? (An outdoor kennel is no place for a Pom, and certainly not a litter – only consider home-reared puppies.)
- What are the breeder's home circumstances? (Will the pup be socialized with children, cats, other dogs, etc.?)
- Will he/she take the puppy back if there are any problems? (Reputable breeders acknowledge their lifetime responsibility to the dogs, and will want any dog to be returned to them if the owner's circumstances change – whatever the dog's age.)

It is important to see the puppies with their mother.

- Will he/she offer advice for as long as the dog lives?

If you are satisfied with the breeder's replies, and the breeder is happy to consider you as a potential owner of one of their dogs, you should arrange to visit in person.

Viewing the litter

It is a good idea to take a friend or family member with you to the breeder. This should stop you from falling head over heels in love with the puppies and making a rash decision. The breeder may also ask to see any children you have, to assess whether they are old enough or sufficiently well behaved to be trusted with a delicate Pom puppy.

When you arrive, look for the following:

- Is the home clean?
- Are the adult dogs healthy and lively?
- Is the litter's dam a good example of a Pom? Is she alert? Good-natured? Would you be happy if the puppy turns out like her? If her coat is in poor condition, do not worry – some coat always falls out after whelping.
- Are the puppies clean? Check for feces, parasites, or flea dirt in the coat, runny eyes, and other obvious signs of ill health.
- Are the puppies a good weight? They should be a little plump but you should not be able to feel their ribs, and there should be no evidence of a potbelly (a sign of worm infestation).
- The puppies should be playful, friendly, alert, and active. Avoid any that are shy, or are the runts of the litter – such puppies will need experienced owners to nurture them.
- If they have just been fed, the puppies may be sleepy; if this is the case, arrange another visit to see them at a different time of the day.

PICKING THE PUP

Male or female?

Your choice of a male or female puppy may be limited, depending on what is available in the litter. Females particularly may be difficult to find (litters are usually small, and the breeder may want to keep a female for his or her own future breeding program).

There are no significant differences between the sexes. Some say that females are more loving, but others dispute this. Bred to be a Toy dog, both sexes are equally affectionate and make superb companions.

Females will come into season, if they are not spayed, which is a consideration (see page 76). Your choice may also depend on whether you already have other dogs (for example, if you have an intact male, then you may want to choose another male, or opt to spay a female puppy).

Color

In theory, there are lots of colors to choose from – black, blue, brown, red, cream, orange, white. As well as the solid colors, these shades also come in parti-color (patches of color), black and tan, and brindle (a red or gold base with black cross stripes). However, in practice, some colors are very rare! The most popular color by far is orange.

By six weeks of age, you should have a good indication of the puppy's eventual coat color. The breeder is likely to look at the base of the ear, which is where the true coat color first shows through. Often a puppy loses his sable coloring as he develops – for example, a lot of adult cream dogs are wolf sables who lost their sable!

Because the changes are hard to predict, your national kennel club will generally accept a change in color quite easily, recognizing that, at the time of registration, the breeder can only make an educated guess.

POM COLORS

The Pomeranian comes in a wide range of colors.

LEFT
Cream Poms are real eye-catchers!

LEFT
Orange: The most common color.

RIGHT
Black is seen in the show ring much more often nowadays.

LEFT
Orange sable (orange and black) is quite common.

RIGHT
Shaded sable: Each hair should be shaded in three colors.

The breeder will help you to assess show potential.

The color changes do not end once a Pom has shed his puppy coat. The color can change slightly every time the dog blows coat (every six months in the case of intact females, and once a year in dogs and spayed females).

Show potential

With such small litters, finding a show-quality puppy can take a lot of patience. Most breeders breed because they want a puppy from two particular dogs. If there is a bitch in the litter, they are likely to keep her for their breeding program. If there is an outstanding dog in the litter, they may keep him too. Since, in most litters, there are just two puppies, that doesn't leave very many to sell!

If you are new to showing, then it is unlikely that you will be very successful with your first dog – whichever puppy you buy.

Most people do their show apprenticeships with their first Pom – and then, by the time they move on to their second show dog, they have some experience under their belts and are likely to have more success. Those who really get bitten by the show bug and want the best-quality dogs then usually become involved in breeding, so they do not have to rely on other people's cast-offs!

If you are a novice, ask the breeder's advice. Tell them you intend to show the dog, and ask if they have a show-quality puppy. Be warned: Breeders are not fortune-tellers. They may be able to tell if a puppy has potential, but there are no guarantees that this potential will be realized as the puppy matures.

A breeder usually holds on to a promising puppy until the age of six months, when they will better be able to tell if the Pom in question has what it takes. Although spotting a good Pomeranian is often second nature to experienced breeders, here are some of the things they will be looking for in an older puppy:

- A good mouth – the puppy should have the correct bite, although when he loses his milk teeth, there is a chance his adult teeth will grow incorrectly. By six months of age, you should be able to tell if the adult bite is correct.
- Two descended testicles in a dog.
- Harshness of coat (avoid a soft coat).
- Correct tail (it should be set high, be kink-free, and curl over the back).
- A show-off temperament (the dog should look confident and proud, and act as if he's the best thing on the planet).

For more details on show-quality Poms, see Chapter Nine.

One's enough!

Don't be tempted to buy two puppies at the same time – indeed, you should be suspicious if a breeder has two to sell so easily, given the small litters in the breed.

Raising a puppy is hard work – all the training and socializing is a full-time job in itself. Two puppies will be double the work, will make training more difficult, and won't give you the time to bond with each dog so easily. If you really want two Pomeranians, wait until the first dog is at least a year old before starting over again with a new one.

PREPARING FOR PUPPY

Once you've booked your puppy, you will have to wait until he is old enough to leave his mother and littermates (usually at 12 weeks of age). In the meantime, you can begin making preparations for his home-coming.

Puppy-proofing

Although they are small and look like the most saintly creatures that ever graced the earth, Pom puppies can be very naughty! They also have the curiosity of the cat, and like to investigate.

Before bringing home your puppy, you should go around your house on your hands and knees to see things from a Pom's perspective. Can you reach the bottom of a hanging tablecloth or any electric cords? Can you reach that knickknack on the coffee table, or that houseplant? Remove all objects that can

The inquisitive Pom will investigate everything, so check that the plants in your garden are dog-friendly.

be knocked over, any that are dangerous if chewed, and those that would upset you if they were munched or urinated on.

You should also make your yard a safe haven. Thoroughly investigate your boundaries. Poms are tiny and can squeeze through the smallest of gaps in fences or under gates, so don't take any chances.

If you have a pond or a swimming pool, make sure the puppy cannot gain access to the water – he could fall in and drown. Make sure your plants and trees are dog-friendly (your garden center can advise you on which ones are toxic – the same applies to houseplants), and make sure that other potential dangers (sharp gardening equipment, pesticides, etc.) are locked away in a shed or garage.

Shopping list
Collar and lead

Being so tiny, Poms are not suited to the traditional leather, buckle collars and matching leads. Not only are they too heavy, but the dog's profuse coat would get tangled up in the fittings. The ideal solution is a slip lead, which is used in the show ring. It loops over the head, and is light enough for the breed, while ensuring the dog cannot run off.

If you are taking your dog out in a public place, such as a park, he should be fitted with a collar and tag (it is a legal obligation in many places). The tag should give your contact details. Choose a light nylon collar and adjust it so that you can easily fit two fingers underneath. Remove the collar as soon as you get home

(otherwise it will gradually wear away the dog's coat), and never leave it on if you cannot supervise your puppy (it could get caught on something and strangle him).

Toys

Poms are very playful dogs and need to be kept mentally stimulated, so buy a good range of durable, safe toys. Your Pom will enjoy chasing after and chewing a small rope toy, or driving everyone mad with a squeaky toy.

Do check that the toys are puppy-friendly, though. Squeaks and other parts can be exposed through repeated chewing. If swallowed, they could cause choking, so check the toys regularly for any sign of damage and replace them if necessary.

Also make sure that the toy is the right size for your Pom – neither large enough to be uninteresting and unmanageable, nor small enough to be swallowed.

Food

Before picking up the puppy, ask the breeder what food the Pom is used to and stock up. It is important not to change the food suddenly, as this can cause tummy upsets (see page 51). Being such a small breed, the Pom has specific nutritional needs and should be fed a good-quality diet, so you are best guided by the breeder.

Crate

This has numerous uses – as the puppy's bed, to hold him securely during car travel, to contain

Make sure the toys you buy are 100 percent safe.

him when he cannot be supervised for short periods, and so on. Although crates look a bit austere, if they are lined with some snug, fleecy bedding, and some safe chews and toys are added, dogs quickly learn to love their own, cozy dens (see also page 40).

Grooming equipment

You will need:

- A double-sided metal comb (one side with narrow teeth and one with wide teeth)
- A good-quality bristle brush with a rubber base
- Cotton swabs to clean the eyes and ears
- A gentle dog shampoo
- Scissors to trim the coat
- Guillotine-type nail clippers
- A child's-size toothbrush
- Canine toothpaste

For more information, see Chapter Five.

Vetting the vet

Choose a veterinarian before you pick up your puppy, and make an appointment for the day after you bring him home. During this visit, the veterinarian will give the puppy a general health check, discuss neutering and basic care with you, and arrange to complete any worming or vaccination programs started by the breeder (don't forget to take along details of any treatments received). During the visit, ask if the clinic runs puppy parties, where young puppies are socialized together in a safe environment.

So where do you start in finding the right veterinarian? Picking one at random from a phone book is not recommended – there will be times when this person will have your Pom's life in their hands. Make sure you choose the best person for such a responsible job! Word-of-mouth recommendations are always the best places to start. Once you have some possibles, arrange to visit each practice and talk to the staff.

- What are the opening hours – do they fit in with your lifestyle? For example, if they are open mornings and afternoons only, can you take your kids to school and still take your dog to the vet?
- What emergency facilities are available? Some offices have a veterinarian on call 24 hours a day; others can refer you to an emergency veterinary hospital.
- Are the staff members friendly, knowledgeable, and caring?
- Is it important to you that holistic treatments are available at the practice?
- Does the practice have adequate parking facilities?
- Is it within easy reach of your home in an emergency?

THE DAY ARRIVES!

You've done all the pre-puppy preparations and finally it is time to pick up your Pom. Try to arrange to get the puppy in the morning. If you have kids, this will enable you to settle your Pom in before the children come home from school. Spending half the day introducing him to his new environment should help him to enjoy a calmer, less stressful first night (see page 33).

It is helpful to take a friend or family member along with you to drive while you hold the puppy. This is preferable to putting the new addition in a crate in the back of the car (he will not only feel isolated, but could also break a limb if he is bumped around in a crate

At last, the great day arrives when it is time to pick up your puppy.

during the journey). Being separated from his human and canine family for the first time, this could be quite a stressful journey for the puppy, so a reassuring cuddle will get your new life together off to a better start.

Before you leave the breeder, make sure you have the puppy's registration details, pedigree, receipt, and so on, as well as a diet sheet (see page 51). It also helps to have a toy or some bedding from his old home – having something familiar will reassure him when he is surrounded by all the sights, sounds, and smells in his new home.

On the journey home, make sure the temperature in the car is neither too hot nor too cold. It must be a comfortable temperature and well ventilated. Put a thick, soft towel on your lap – not only will it be more cozy, it will also be useful if the puppy has an accident or is carsick (as new puppies often are). If it is a long trip, regularly offer him water.

CHAPTER THREE

SETTLING IN

So, after all your planning and preparation, you finally have your Pomeranian puppy home! Everyone in the family is bound to be excited to meet him, but it is important to remain calm and not to overwhelm him. After leaving his home and family (canine and human), he will need a few days to get used to the change of environment and to settle in before being introduced to neighbors, friends, and your extended family.

When you first get your puppy home, you should take him outside – after the journey, he may need to relieve himself (see page 39). After he's done his business, take him indoors and let him have a sniff around one or two of the rooms. Initially, it's best if he doesn't come into contact with other pets in the family. Keep him in a separate part of the house from the other animals for a couple of hours, until he has settled in a little. (For pet introductions, see page 29.)

If he's due for a meal, feed him, take him outside again, then perhaps introduce him to his bed and see if he will take a nap. Although it may seem as if puppies are always on the go, they actually need a surprising amount of sleep.

FAMILY INTRODUCTIONS

Child's play

As previously discussed, breeders are very careful about where they place their dogs – particularly when children are present. This is for a very good reason: Poms are tiny, delicate dogs who can be seriously injured – even killed – if dropped, fallen on, stepped on, etc. It is therefore imperative, even if you have impeccably behaved children or grandchildren, to teach them what is acceptable, even before bringing the puppy home.

• Boisterous play is forbidden when the puppy is in the same room or yard. A Pom puppy

Janice Moore, from Suffolk, England, is a breeder with extensive experience of Poms and children. She feels strongly that, far from them being incompatible, they can become the very best of friends.

"I've had German Shepherds for 40 years, and Poms for nine. I now have about 30 Poms, which I breed and show. They might seem a strange combination at first, but they are both essentially herding dogs, and have very similar temperaments. Both love people, though the herding aspect means they are reserved and wary of strangers at first.

"Ryan, my grandson, is nine years old, so he has grown up with the Poms. My son and daughter-in-law both work. I look after him occasionally, and have done since he was a baby. He knows all the dogs' names – something most adults can't remember!

SMILEY POMS

"From the first time that the Poms met Ryan, they loved him. They somehow knew to be gentle with him. As he grew, so they stayed friends. When he was a toddler, they would dive on him and lick him all over if he fell.

"The dogs become all 'smiley' when Ryan visits. Tanny Anne, my older bitch, particularly idolizes him. She and Ryan are similar ages, so they've known each other all their lives. Even my male Poms, who don't generally tolerate younger pups, enjoy Ryan's company.

"Little dogs are only nasty with children – or adults – if they are treated nastily. If they trust their human family, and are respected, there should be no problems at all.

"The only time they were wary of Ryan was when he was around three to five years, and a little unpredictable. He once started jumping around the dogs, and I immediately told him to stop and explained that the dogs were frightened of him instead of loving him. He remembered that and would always calm himself down if he started to get overexcited again.

"My friend has four children, who have also grown up around my dogs. Aidan, aged four, fell backwards a couple of months ago, and the Poms all dived on him and licked him all over – even in his ears! Aidan was in hysterics, and couldn't get up for laughing.

"Poms are lively, fun dogs. If they were human, they would be clowns, because they revel in making people laugh. They have that love of life that children also have."

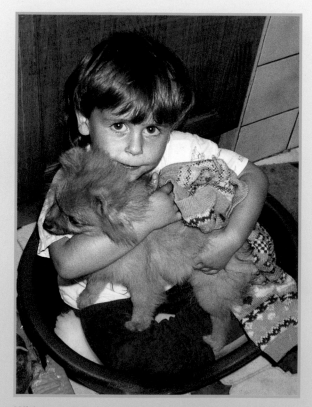

With sensible supervision, there is no reason why children and Poms cannot become the best of friends.

A perfect match: These dogs have grown up together, and are great companions.

can easily be killed by being stepped on accidentally.

- Teasing is another no-no – the dog must always be treated with respect and kindness. A Pom has a long memory and will bear a grudge for many years.
- The dog should be left to eat in peace; when he goes to his bed, he should not be disturbed.
- Children should not pick up the puppy – if dropped, he could be seriously (possibly fatally) injured. If they want to hold the puppy, they must first sit down on the floor.
- Cuddles should be gentle – a Pom can be killed by a vigorous squeeze.
- Children and dogs should always be supervised – especially when the breed is as small and fragile as a Pom. Children can

easily tire a puppy through too much play, or could become overexcited and accidentally hurt him.

RESIDENT DOG

Poms think they are big dogs. In their heads and their hearts they are – it's just their bodies that are small! A Pom will play with a much larger dog without a care in the world, but care must be taken. If you have a boisterous, adolescent Labrador Retriever, for instance, or a large Great Dane, use your common sense. If your dog is likely to run into your Pom or accidentally step on him, heartbreak could result. You should wait until your other dog has grown up and is more sedate, or, if your dog is a perpetual puppy at heart, consider not having a Pom at all.

GREEN-EYED MONSTER

Poms are people dogs through and through. Their whole reason for living is their owner, so introducing a newcomer can be tricky. In a Pom's head, this is a rival for your lap!

Feed them separately, because most dog fights occur over food (you can also end up with one dog who bolts his food and then nudges the slower eater out of the way and eats that meal too!).

Toys, beds, and other possessions can also spark a quarrel. Make sure each dog has his own bed/crate, and do not introduce new toys when the dogs are together. Bring them out for the dogs to play with separately. When they have settled with each other, this rule can be relaxed.

It is also important to give lots of attention to your older dog. When raising a puppy, it is easy to neglect an adult dog, so set time aside to cuddle and play with him to make sure he doesn't resent the new puppy.

Make sure you give both equal attention so jealousies do not arise.

The most hotly contested area will be you! A Pom can get very jealous if another dog is having a cuddle and he is left out. Even if you put both dogs on your lap, fights can erupt over who is closest to you! Rather than trying to balance one dog on each knee (impossible if you have three or more dogs!), make sure you give each dog his own time to enjoy being petted all alone.

If you have an old, calm, or small dog, and you are certain he can be trusted with a tiny Pom, then they are quite likely to become the best of friends.

Toy dogs
Introduce the two dogs outside, in your yard. Your established dog is likely to feel less territorial here than in "his" house.

- If your older dog is a Pom or another Toy breed, pick him up and cuddle him. Then kneel down and encourage the new puppy to come over. They can both sniff each other and get themselves acquainted without the older dog being jealous and without the puppy coming to any harm.

- If either dog growls, tell him "No!" firmly, so he learns that he cannot be bad-tempered with his new housemate.
- When they have had a sniff, let both dogs investigate each other on the ground.
- They may be wary at first, but, with time, will soon get used to each other.
- Never leave them unsupervised, unless you are certain that they can be trusted.

Larger dogs

- As above, the first meeting should take place in your yard.
- If introducing a Pom to a larger dog, whom you cannot hold, put the big dog on a lead so you have control over him.
- Hold the puppy and let your other dog come over and have a sniff.
- As before, reprimand the dog or puppy if there is any growling.
- When your older dog has investigated the new arrival, put the puppy on the ground and let them get to know each other. Do not let your dog off the lead until you are sure that no harm can come to the puppy.
- Speak to both dogs in a calm, reassuring tone, telling them what good dogs they are.

Keep the initial introduction short and sweet. Take the dogs indoors, separate them, and feed them (or give them a treat). They will learn to associate these meetings with a rewarding experience if they end with a treat. After the meal/treat, give your older dog oodles of attention to avoid any feelings of insecurity or jealousy, and try another meeting in a couple of hours. After a few days of short, frequent meetings, where both dogs learn that the other isn't a threat, the novelty will soon wear off. They will settle down to life together, either merely tolerating each other or becoming good friends and playmates.

COOL CATS

You shouldn't have any trouble introducing a Pom to a household where there is a cat. Being so small, Poms rarely threaten a cat, and they generally settle in together quickly.

Of course, every dog and cat is different, and you will improve your chances of domestic peace and harmony if you choose a puppy that has been reared in a home with cats, because he will be used to them from the very start.

Introduce the pair in a room where all doors and windows are shut, but where the cat has something high that she can perch on if she wants to get away from the puppy (for example, the back of the sofa or the windowsill).

Cats like routine, so there could be a lot of fluffing and hissing when the two meet. Never force the two together – the cat will feel trapped and will lash out. It is best simply to supervise them in the same room together, until they eventually just get used to each other.

As dog and cat breeder Eve Smail explains, "The cat will sit for days and days, waiting for the puppy to go away. Then comes the realization that the puppy is here to stay and that she will just have to get used to it."

When curiosity gets the better of the cat (or she

MOTHER LOVE

Eve Smail from Midlothian, Scotland, has had a lifetime with Poms and cats. A kennel and cattery owner, she has had more experience than most ensuring that her cats and dogs do not fight like…well, cats and dogs!

"My Poms have grown up having cats around. If brought up together as puppies and kittens, they know no different. Kittens accept dogs as part of the feline family and will do to a puppy what they would do to each other – rub against them, clean their faces, and groom them.

"However, cats always have the upper hand! If a dog gets overexcited, a cat has no hesitation in giving them a swipe and putting them in their place.

"I breed Burmese and Siamese cats, and have bred Persians in the past. I find that purebred cats generally get along better with dogs than mixed-breed cats do. This is especially true of dog-like cats, such as Siamese, Tonkinese, and Burmese.

FERAL INSTINCT

"Ordinary mixed-breed cats still have quite a wild, feral instinct, and it can be pot luck whether they take to a dog. Purebred dogs – and certainly Poms – have virtually lost that wildness through many years of selective breeding. Purebred cats are also more domesticated; they are invariably kept indoors, and, over several generations, their instincts become diluted.

"That said, one of the most special moments between my animals has involved a cat and a Pom. Sheba is a three-legged mixed breed (she lost her leg in a traffic accident but recovered fully). She produced three kittens a few days before one of my Poms, Tots,

produced three puppies. Unfortunately, Tots had a problem with her milk. In desperation, we put some kitten urine on the puppies and snuggled them underneath the kittens as Sheba was nursing them. They fed from her – and she let them.

"Cats suckle far longer than dogs – kittens don't seem to use their teeth, whereas puppies do, so Sheba did very well to feed them for three and a half weeks. She not only fed them, but also cleaned and groomed them (but she never cleaned their bottoms!).

KITTEN CARE

"When the puppies approached four weeks of age, we took over, giving them solid food. We separated them from Sheba and the kittens, and put them in a pen next door. Still, Sheba would go and visit them – leaping into the pen, licking their heads and faces, and then returning to her 'proper' kittens!

"All the Poms love Sheba. When they see her, they run up to her and mob her, licking her all over. She'll take so much, but after a while, out comes the paw as if to say, 'Enough's enough! Calm down!'

"My new American import, Am/Can Ch. Foxworth Fun and Games at Toybox (the name is bigger than the dog!), wasn't used to cats when he came here. When he saw Sheba, he got very excited – I think he wanted to murder her! When he raced up to her, she remained still and he didn't know what to do! He was used to cats running away and then chasing them. You could see the look in Sheba's eye. She was coolly saying, 'I don't run.' Because he didn't get a reaction from her, the fascination has gone and he pretty much ignores her now. Sheba won't stand for any nonsense from any dog!"

Sabel, a female Maine Coon Cat, is perfectly happy to share her home with Marco, a male Pom.

is resigned to having to cohabit with a dog), puss will probably get fairly close to the puppy, have a sniff, and may hiss just to show who's boss!

"Pom pups are braver than their physiology permits – much bolder than is good for them," says Eve. If a puppy does yap at a cat, a quick swipe soon puts a stop to any impertinent behavior! It is a good idea, therefore, to clip the cat's nails before any introductions, to avoid any serious injury.

Some cats take to the newcomer quickly, and many Poms and cats groom each other and sleep together. Other cats never fully accept the dog, but will learn to tolerate the new housemate.

Although a hands-off approach is recommended, never leave the two animals unsupervised until they are perfectly happy with each other. A Pom puppy is so tiny that he could easily be killed by a hunting cat, so do not take any chances.

Introducing a kitten to an established Pom is also straightforward - the kitten will accept the Pom right from the start because she won't know any different. She may fluff herself up a bit for the first few encounters, but she will soon realize that the Pom is a friend, not a foe – and is also a very warm, soft, fluffy bedmate!

FIRST NIGHT

After a long day, picking up the puppy, introducing him to his new home and family, and making sure he is fed, watered, and taken outside throughout the day, you'll be looking forward to a good, long sleep. Think again!

The first night (or two, or three, or more, depending on the puppy), may be noisy, so warn any neighbors in advance. This may sound a little dramatic – after all, Pom pups are tiny.

CHAPTER FOUR

EARLY LESSONS

Many people make the mistake of thinking that the Pom is a pretty little airhead – sweet, loving, glamorous, but as short in brains as he is in height! What little they know! Poms must be one of the smartest of all Toy breeds. They have not just inherited the appearance of their smart, working spitz cousins (see Chapter One), but also their intelligence.

Poms are fast learners and enthusiastic pupils. They will especially love their training sessions because it means spending quality time with their dear owner. As you've probably realized by now, Poms revel in being the center of attention!

Once your puppy has mastered the basics in this chapter, why not consider more advanced training when he is a little older? There are lots of ideas in Chapter Seven, and you are bound to find something that suits you and your dog.

NAME GAME

Decide on a name early on – preferably before you bring your puppy home. Then you can begin using it right from the start. Choose something that is short and easy to say – a longer name will only be shortened over time anyway.

Initially, teach your puppy his name by saying it in a happy tone of voice and then giving him a treat. This way, he will learn to associate his name with enjoyable experiences, and is more likely to respond to it in the future.

PACK POSITION

Dogs are pack animals, and from the minute you bring your Pom home, he will try to find his position in his new human "pack." The secret to successful lifelong training is to establish yourself as leader of that pack. This is far easier to achieve when your Pom is still a puppy, because he will naturally be more subservient.

- Feed your puppy after your family has eaten. In the wild, each dog eats in order of importance.
- Only give your puppy half his meal. When he is close to finishing, take the bowl from him and add the remainder. This will teach him not to become possessive over his food. He will learn that you provide and take away food as you see fit, and, by your adding the occasional treat, he will learn that your interference is to be welcomed.

Teach your puppy to understand "No!" and you will save yourself a lot of trouble.

- When your puppy is playing with a toy, take it from him, give him a treat and then return the toy. If he will not let go, attract his attention with the treat (he will probably prefer a tasty morsel to a toy), command "Give," and wait until he gives you the toy. Only then give him the treat and praise him enthusiastically. Repeat this exercise several times a day until your Pom will give you the toy whenever you ask.
- When you play with your Pom, make sure it is you who decides when the game is over and that it is you who has possession of the toy when the game is finished.

- If your puppy bites you during play, say "No!" in as stern a voice as possible (see below), and ignore your puppy until he learns to play without biting. Most puppies mouth their owners and they do not intend to hurt, but you need to establish early on that it is not acceptable.
- Involve all the family in the above exercises, so that your Pom learns he is subservient to everyone, including children. If you do not have any children, try to borrow some from family, friends, or neighbors.

THE POSITIVE NEGATIVE!

Whether you want to prevent him from jumping up on people or to stop him chewing your new shoes, teaching your Pom to understand "No!" will save you a lot of trouble.

The secret to a successful "No!" is to sound as if you really mean it. Be as stern as possible, using a tone that makes it clear you mean business. Never relent. Once you have said "No!" you must stick to it. If you back down, your puppy will quickly learn that he can get his way if he persists long enough.

If your puppy ignores you, do not overreact or he will learn that disobedience is a great way to get your attention. Instead, ignore him. For example, if your puppy jumps up on you, turn your back on him and ignore him until he is quiet, with all four paws on the floor. Only then turn around and reward him, praising him for his good behavior. He will soon get the idea.

HOUSETRAINING

Housetraining is relatively straightforward, provided you follow some simple rules and remember to be vigilant. If you do your job correctly, you will never be faced with cleaning up one of those little accidents again.

The first step is to decide where you would like your puppy to relieve himself, such as a spot in the corner of the yard. During the first few hours after you bring your puppy home, you should take him to this spot so that he becomes familiar with it.

Regular routine

Having decided on your puppy's toileting area, you need to establish a regular routine. Remember, while your puppy is still very young, he will need to relieve himself quite often. If you do not give your puppy enough chances to do this, you only have yourself to blame if he has an accident in the house.

Take your puppy outside at the following times:
- As soon as he wakes up
- Before and after excitement (play sessions, for example, or meeting new people)

Establish a routine of taking your puppy out at regular intervals, and he will soon learn to be clean in the house.

- After eating
- Before and after sleeping
- Last thing at night
- Every two hours

If your puppy does not eliminate immediately when you take him to his spot, wait until he does. If he has not gone within ten minutes, take him back inside and try again half an hour later. Some dogs will try to postpone relieving themselves because they are reluctant to return to the house – the yard is a big adventure waiting to be explored. To overcome this problem, it helps to have a play session after your puppy has relieved himself. This way, he learns that "performing" when you want him to results in a reward, rather than the end of his fun.

Using a phrase, such as "Be busy," will help your puppy to learn to relieve himself when you want him to. Wait until he starts to go, and then say "Be busy." Once your puppy has had all his inoculations, you can ask him to "Be busy" when you take him for a walk. He will soon learn to relieve himself at convenient times. Remember that whatever phrase you use, you will have to use it in public, so it is best to choose something fairly innocuous.

Accidents happen

You can avoid many accidents by watching your puppy closely. If he starts sniffing the ground, circling or squatting, or if he tries to find a quiet corner to hide in, he probably needs to relieve himself and you will need to act quickly.

Clap your hands loudly to startle your Pom and make him stop whatever he is doing. Whisk him away to his spot as quickly as possible, remember to use your chosen phrase, and reward him when he performs.

If, despite your best efforts, your puppy has an accident in the house, do not scold him. He will not associate your bad mood with his accident and will only feel hurt and bewildered. Accidents are a part of owning a puppy, and are only to be expected. It is not your puppy's fault and you will simply have to be more vigilant in the future.

CRATE TRAINING

It is recommended that you buy a crate for your Pomeranian puppy (see page 23). As well as somewhere safe to sleep at night, a crate is a great way of keeping your puppy out of mischief during the day.

Make the crate as comfortable as possible and fill it with safe chew toys. A great choice is a boredom-busting toy, such as a chew bone with enticing bits of food inside. Make sure your puppy has relieved himself before putting him in the crate.

Initially, your puppy should not remain inside his crate for more than half an hour at a time. Regular, short sessions such as these will teach your puppy to be calm in your absence. This will help avoid problems later, such as separation anxiety. You must establish the crate as a quiet, safe haven – somewhere your puppy can play undisturbed – rather than a place he associates with punishment or boredom.

ACCEPTING GROOMING

You should establish good grooming habits while your Pom is still a pup, so that you both become accustomed to the routine.

Early sessions

To begin with, do your grooming in a very informal manner. Use a soft-bristled brush, and while the puppy is on your lap having a cuddle, gently stroke him all over with the brush. You should find that he quickly begins to enjoy the sensation.

Once he is used to being brushed, roll the puppy on his back and groom his tummy and tail gently. If you remain calm and persistent, remembering to talk to your puppy encouragingly throughout and to praise him lavishly when he consents to being groomed, you should not have too many problems. You must teach your puppy that grooming is an enjoyable experience rather than a chore.

If your puppy objects strenuously, trying to bite you or the brush, tell him "No!" as firmly as possible and continue. Never use the brush to

Encourage your puppy to settle in his crate for short sessions to begin with.

punish the puppy. Gentle persistence will achieve far better results than brute force.

Keep the sessions very short – about five minutes. As your puppy's coat grows, you can extend the sessions and use a brush with firmer bristles, eventually progressing to a comb. Always end each session with praise, a treat, or play, so that your puppy learns that cooperation brings rewards.

Learning to stand

Once your Pom has become accustomed to being brushed on your lap, you should teach him to stand while being groomed.

- Choose a spot where you will groom your puppy and stick to it. You want your puppy to associate that spot with being groomed, so that he knows what is expected of him.
- Gather your grooming equipment and have it ready on hand.
- Place your puppy on the table and put him in the *stand* position. Say the word "*Stand,*" praise him, and give him a treat. Never turn your back on the puppy once he is on the table, because he could jump off and hurt himself.

HANDLING

It is important that a puppy learns to accept handling all over.

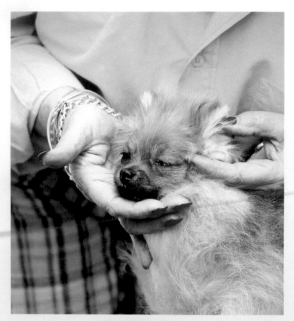

Check the ears.

Examine the teeth.

Pick up each paw in turn.

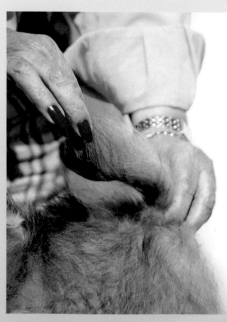

Lift up the tail.

- Practice this for a few minutes each day, until your puppy is standing reliably. Do not expect him to stand for too long – he will become bored and stop cooperating.
- Over the next two to three months, train him to stand for longer periods, so that by the time his adult coat has grown, he will stand for as long as needed for grooming.

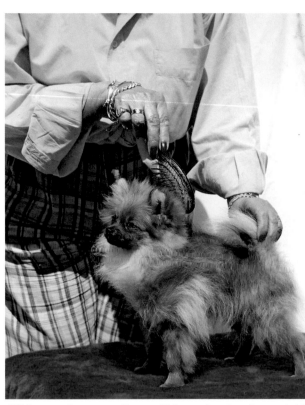

With practice, your Pom will learn to stand on a table while he is being groomed.

Access all areas

When teaching your puppy to accept grooming, it is essential that you touch him from the tip of his nose to the tip of his tail. Your Pom must learn to accept being touched all over. This is particularly important if you plan to show your Pom (see Chapter Nine), and it is also essential for visits to the veterinarian, not to mention the fact that it will make your life a lot easier.

At the end of each session, always give him a treat so your Pom associates grooming with enjoyment.

Feet

While you are grooming your pup, pick up each of his feet in turn and hold them for a few moments, remembering to touch the areas around the nails so that your puppy will accept nail-clipping at a later date.

Face, eyes, and ears

The face should be included in your grooming routine, with particular attention paid to the eyes. Use a moustache comb (which is smaller than combs used elsewhere on the coat) to untangle the facial hair.

You should accustom your Pom to having his eyes wiped. There are solutions on the market for this, but a mild, very dilute solution of salt or baking soda and water works just as well (see page 58).

Also remember to feel the inside and outside of the ears, cleaning them if necessary (see page 59).

Teeth

Do not forget to include teeth-cleaning during grooming (page 59). If you get him used to it now, it will be easier to do in the future.

COLLAR COMFORT

There is nothing worse than going for a walk with a dog that does not know how to behave on a lead. However, this need never be a problem, provided you accustom your Pom to wearing a collar and being on a lead when he is still a puppy.

You will need to buy a soft collar suitable for a small breed like the Pomeranian. Remember that wearing a collar for extended periods will cause a dent in your Pom's ruff, because the collar will gradually wear away the fur. Consequently, most Pom owners use a slip lead, with a very lightweight tag attached for the owner's name and telephone number, etc.

Initially, put the collar on your puppy for no more than a few minutes at a time. As soon as you have put it on, praise your puppy and keep him distracted by playing a game with him. Gradually increase the length of time the puppy wears the collar until he is able to keep it on comfortably for the length of time he will be on a walk.

Early lead-training should involve no more than a quick wander around the yard with your Pom on the lead. Encourage your puppy to remain at your side by talking to him reassuringly. Most Poms prefer to be at their owner's side rather than racing off ahead. However, if your puppy pulls, call him back and refuse to move until he returns to your side. Never shout at him or yank on the lead.

SOCIALIZATION

Once your puppy is protected by his puppy vaccinations and can walk on the lead, it's time to go out into the big, wide world. One of the joys of owning a Toy breed is that they can accompany you to most places. It is therefore important that your puppy be socialized from a young age so that he grows into a happy, well-mannered dog who is confident in all environments.

Be imaginative about where you take him, to ensure he will encounter many different situations. Here are some ideas.

When your puppy is walking happily on a lead you can venture into the wide world.

- Take him to a shopping center, and just sit and watch the world go by. There, he will see all types and ages of people, wheelchairs, strollers, etc.
- Carry him along a busy street.
- Visit friends and relatives.
- Take a trip on public transportation, or visit a bus or train station.

Be confident in all these places, and your Pom will learn there is nothing to be afraid of. Give him a treat every now and again when he is not reacting to what is going on around him. If he shows fear, reassure him, but do not fuss over him, or he will think there is something to worry about. (Some dogs also learn to feign fear, knowing that they will get lots of attention!) Just behave matter-of-factly, and carry on as normal.

TRAINING EXERCISES

Fortunately, the Pom is a very people-oriented breed who loves nothing more than his owner's undivided attention, and this will work to your advantage when training him.

   Keep training sessions short and fun, and use a reward that most motivates your dog, e.g., a cuddle, food, or a game. If you use food as a training prop, remember to deduct the quantity from your dog's main meal, otherwise you will quickly end up with a very fat Pom!

Sit

Sit is one of the first exercises you should teach your puppy. A dog that will sit on

If your Pom is exposed to a variety of situations, he will become well adjusted.

command can be taken nearly everywhere, because it is a great way of keeping him out of trouble.

- Hold a treat in your hand. Show it to your Pom.
- You should find that your puppy follows your hand with his head.
- Slowly bring your hand just above your pup's head, so that he has to lean back in the *sit* position to reach the treat.
- As soon as his bottom hits the floor, say "*Sit*" and give him the treat.
- Do not be surprised if your puppy tries to jump up to get the treat, or if he starts

Use a treat to encourage your puppy to sit.

barking. It will take him a while to realize what he must do, but he will get there eventually.

- Practice little and often, until your Pom will sit on the voice command alone. However, always give him a treat from time to time to keep him interested.

- Incorporate the *sit* into your Pom's everyday life. Ask him to sit before you give him his food bowl or put on his lead, etc. The more he practices, the more reliable he will be.

- Once your Pom has learned to sit reliably at home and in his normal routine, you should begin asking him to sit when there are other distractions, such as when he is out on a walk and happily engrossed in sniffing. The aim is to have a dog that will sit on command, every time you ask, wherever he may be.

Down

The *down* is really an extension of the *sit*. A dog that is in the *down* position is less likely to get up and wander than a dog in the *sit*, so *down* is an extremely advantageous exercise to learn.

- Ask your Pom to sit.
- Show him a treat and slowly bring it down so that it is just in front of his paws.
- He is likely to stoop down to reach the treat, but you must not let him have it until his body is flat on the floor.
- When your Pom eventually lies down correctly, say "*Down*," give him the treat, and praise him.
- Keep practicing until your Pom will go into the *down* without the need for a treat. However, as with the *sit*, remember to give the occasional treat to keep your puppy's interest.
- As with the *sit*, try to incorporate the exercise into your Pom's daily routine, and begin to introduce a variety of distractions.

Start from the sit, *and lower a treat to encourage your puppy to go* down.

Come

This is probably the most important exercise you will ever teach your Pomeranian. Owning a dog that will come when called is a pleasure, and it is also essential for your dog's safety. If he runs off during a walk, you can stop him from running across a busy road – and possibly being involved in an accident.

The *come,* which is often referred to as the *recall,* is surprisingly easy to teach – particularly to the Pomeranian, who loves to be near his owner. The key is to start young. From eight weeks to five or six months of age is the ideal window of opportunity. After this time, your Pom will become more independent, and the *recall* will be far harder to teach.

• Ask a friend, family member, or neighbor to help you with this exercise.

• Ask your assistant to kneel on the floor, keeping the puppy close in a *sit* position.

• Sit a short distance in front of your puppy and call him to you, by saying your dog's name followed by the word "*Come!*"

• Try to inject as much enthusiasm as possible into your voice, look at your puppy, and hold your arms out wide as if to embrace him. You must look and sound very excited to see your puppy. It may help if you hold a treat in your hand or your Pom's favorite toy.

• You should find that your puppy races over to you. When he arrives, praise him lavishly. Give him a cuddle and a treat and tell him what a good boy he is.

• Practice little and often, gradually increasing the distance your puppy has to travel before

Be ready to reward a response to the come *command.*

he reaches you. Always remember to shower him with praise when he comes to you.

• Once your Pom can perform the *recall* reliably, it is time to start calling him when he cannot see you. Play hide-and-seek games in your home – hide behind the sofa, for example – so that your pup has to track you down.

• Never let your Pom off-lead in a public place until he is performing the *recall* with 100 percent reliability. Until that time, keep him on a Flexi-lead.

- Never shout at your puppy if he fails to come to you or if he takes a long time to arrive. You want him to associate coming to you with being rewarded. If he expects to be shouted at, he will not come at all!

Stay

The *stay* is probably the most difficult exercise to teach. The Pom's love of people is great for teaching the *recall*, but it makes teaching the *stay* more difficult. You need to demonstrate to your Pom that he will be rewarded with extra time in your company if he stays when asked.

- Ask your Pom to "*Sit.*"
- Say "*Stay*" with as much authority as you can muster, and put your hand out in front of you with your palm facing forward (a little like a policeman stopping traffic, but with your hand angled more toward your dog).

Build up the stay exercise in easy stages.

- Wait no more than a few seconds and then reward your dog for staying put.
- Practice this a few times.
- Next, ask your Pom to lie "*Down*," take a step back, and ask him to "*Stay*." After about three seconds, step forward and reward him. Give him a cuddle and make him feel really pleased with himself.
- Gradually increase the length and the distance of the *stay*. Remember to intersperse the exercise with lots of play, so that your Pom does not become bored.
- If your Pom looks as though he may get up and come to you, remind him to stay by giving the command and your hand signal. This may be enough to keep him where he is.

- If your Pom breaks the *stay*, go back a step, decreasing the distance and the time he must stay. Time and distance should be increased very gradually – do not push for too much too quickly.
- Once your Pom has mastered the *down-stay*, you should teach the *sit-stay*, which is exactly the same but with the dog in the *sit* position. Dogs are more likely to break the *sit-stay* because it takes less effort to get up from a *sit* than it does a *down*. However, with patience and practice, not forgetting plenty of praise and rewards, your Pom should soon master the *sit-stay*.

CHAPTER FIVE

CARING FOR A POMERANIAN

Tiny he might be, but, like any dog, the Pom still needs a fair amount of regular care to keep him healthy, happy, and looking simply divine.

FEEDING

As with feeding a puppy, you should feed your adult dog the type and quantity of food recommended by the breeder. He or she will have years of experience as to what achieves the best results in the breed, and so is the best person to be guided by.

If you find the diet does not agree with your dog, or if you are having difficulty getting the recommended brand, consult your dog's breeder, or, failing that, your veterinarian, for suggested alternatives.

As for the number of meals you should feed – again, be guided by the breeder (or rescue organization) that the Pom came from. Some owners feed once a day; most owners of Toy breeds feed two (sometimes three) meals a day.

Some manufacturers make food specifically for Toy dogs. Not only are they small, bite-sized pieces (ideal for tiny jaws), but they contain just the right levels of nutrients for a small dog's specific needs.

When changing a dog's diet, patience is the key. The substitution should be done gradually, over the course of a couple of weeks, to avoid tummy upsets. You should replace a very small part of your dog's ordinary food with a little of the new food. Over the course of about 14 days, gradually increase the amount of new food, and decrease the old food until the food has been completely changed.

Obesity

Many Poms are fussy about what they eat (this common problem is dealt with on page 75). Others relish their food. For this latter group (or those fussy eaters who train their owners to feed them only unhealthy foods), obesity can be a problem – putting undue pressure on the heart and joints (leading to mobility problems and even premature death).

It is very easy to indulge a dog – but especially so with a breed as beautiful as the Pom. When you have one sitting at your side, looking up adoringly at you as you eat a cookie, it takes the willpower of a saint not to break off a piece and give it to him.

However, ignore him you must – otherwise he will always expect such treats, and, before you know it, your once tiny, foxy companion will have a serious weight problem.

Identifying a problem is the first step – the weight creeps on slowly, and it is often difficult to notice when you live with the dog. Most owners are alerted to the fact of canine obesity at their annual routine veterinary visit.

The Pom presents a particular difficulty in that his thick coat can hide a multitude of sins! Remember – although the Pom should appear round from every angle, he shouldn't actually be round! Beneath the coat, there should be a well-shaped body, with ribs that can be felt (but are not prominent), and a visible waist.

- Every week, when you thoroughly groom your dog, feel his body and assess his shape.
- Weigh him weekly. Stand on the scales, weigh yourself, and then weigh yourself again while carrying your dog. Deduct the first figure from the second and you have your Pom's weight. If the weight starts creeping up, feed him a little less to get it back under control.
- If you suspect your Pom is overweight, consult your veterinarian. This is a problem veterinarians see all the time.

- If you want to give your Pom a treat, don't give him a cookie – give him a carrot or a piece of cauliflower. Dogs love vegetables, and they are a much healthier option.

EXERCISE AND PLAY

The Pom is a canine conundrum. He's one of the smallest breeds, yet he descends from large, hardy working dogs. Many people are attracted to the Pomeranian for this very reason – that he is a larger-than-life character in a small body.

It is tempting to think that, being so tiny, the Pom doesn't need any exercise – that everyday life provides sufficient exercise. However, going outdoors provides so much more than physical exercise – it gives opportunities for ongoing socialization and mental stimulation.

Whether you take your dog for a quick walk to buy a newspaper, or for some energetic play in the yard, or even for a five-mile hike, he will accompany you with enthusiasm. He will relish investigating all the new smells, meeting new friends (human and dog), and just being out and about with his beloved owner.

The Pom is one of those breeds that can take as little or as much exercise as you can give. If it's pouring rain and you skip a walk, he won't become manic and tear around the house because he is bored and full of pent-up energy. On the other hand, if you're in the mood for a long walk on the weekend, he is more than capable of keeping up (and can often outwalk his owners!).

The Pom is a lively dog, and play sessions will keep your dog fit and mentally active.

Play is also important for keeping your Pom active and mentally sharp. Poms are intelligent dogs who like to use their brains – they enjoy training, and also like games that challenge their gray matter. Teach him some basic obedience exercises (page 45), perhaps consider taking up a canine sport (Chapter Seven), or just be inventive in the games you play together. For example, hide your dog's favorite toy, ask him to find it and then slowly increase the level of difficulty until he is hunting all around the room or yard like a miniature Bloodhound!

The hair on the chest is brushed in an upward direction.

It is important to brush through to the undercoat.

The feathering on the back of the leg needs particular attention.

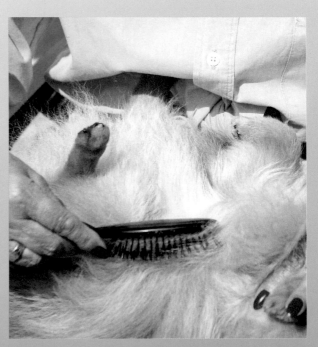

It is easier to groom the Pom's undercarriage if he is lying on your lap.

The profuse coat that grows on the hindquarters is sometimes called the trousers.

The feathering on the underside of the tail is brushed so that it will fan out when it lies flat on the back.

Once brushing is completed, the whole process is repeated using a comb.

GROOMING

The Pom's crowning glory is his coat, but his glamorous good looks are not achieved effortlessly – it is your job to attend to the coat regularly. However, this shouldn't be considered a chore – most owners find it quite a relaxing experience, and, if your puppy has been accustomed to being groomed from an early age, he should enjoy it too. In wild dogs, members of the pack groom each other as a way of bonding and reinforcing relationships – your Pom is likely to view it the same way, and will look forward to his special, quality time with his owner.

Brushing

The leg, chest, tail, back, and neck hair is brushed upward, toward the head. The head hair is also brushed upward. The hair along the tummy is brushed downward, toward the ground, and the hair along the sides of the body (ribs and flanks) is brushed outward so that it stands at 90 degrees to the body.

You should be creating an overall impression of roundness – so that the dog looks like a ball from every angle.

When brushing, make sure you also get through the undercoat – otherwise you will just be tickling the topcoat, while painful mats develop underneath. Do not be so vigorous that you scratch the dog's skin, however.

Once the coat is tangle-free, work through the coat with a wide-tooth comb, and then a narrow-tooth one.

Mat matters

If you encounter a mat, you should try to tease it out gently with the end of a comb and your fingers. Never pull – you will yank the hair out completely. This will not only be painful to your dog, but it will also take some time for the hair to grow back.

There are various mat removers on the market – some of which are remarkably good. Your dog's breeder or a grooming supply shop should be able to guide you; otherwise, you will just have to find the best through trial and error. Usually, you spray the mat with the grooming solution, leave it for a set amount of time, and then gently brush it out.

If there really is no way to untangle a knot, you will have to cut it out. To save as much hair as possible, and to avoid being left with a big hole in the coat, cut the knot lengthwise, not straight across. After every snip, gently brush the area to remove the loose hair and to assess if more needs cutting.

Of course, the best way of dealing with mats is to prevent them. A good daily brush is all that is needed to keep them at bay.

Bathing

This should be done only as necessary, because frequent bathing will remove all the natural oils and will soften what should be a harsh coat (see Chapter Nine). Some show dogs are bathed every week before being exhibited; others hardly ever see the bathroom.

If your Pom just has muddy feet or a dirty bottom, wash the areas with a warm, wet washcloth. If he has rolled in something disgusting and cannot be wiped clean, then you have no option other than to bathe him.

- Before you start, clean the dog's ears, eyes and nails (see pages 58–60).
- Get all the equipment you need close to hand – a plastic pitcher or shower attachment that fits on the faucet, a towel, a good-quality bristle brush, a comb, shampoo, and a saucer.
- Brush and comb the dog thoroughly so there are no tangles in the coat. If a knot is left in, it will be ten times worse to remove after bathing.
- The Pom is small enough to fit in a sink. This will save you bending over a bath – which is backbreaking work (kneeling by the side of the bath doesn't allow you to reach the dog very easily). However, never leave him unattended for a second – if he tried to leap from the sink, he could fall and injure himself badly.
- Run a couple of inches of warm water into the sink, and stand your dog in it.
- Wet the coat thoroughly, using the pitcher or shower attachment. Do the head last, and make sure you do not pour water directly over his face (this may unnerve him).
- When the coat is wet through (make sure you have got through the thick undercoat and down to the skin), put a little warm water in a saucer and mix in some shampoo.
- Apply this solution with your hands all over the coat, and massage it with your fingertips right down to the skin. Make sure no soapy suds get into your dog's eyes.
- Rinse thoroughly with clean, warm (not hot) water. Make sure you shield the eyes as you rinse the head.

- Now rinse again – it is crucial that no trace of shampoo is left in the coat.
- Never use a conditioner – it might make brushing the coat a little easier, but it will soften it, which is highly undesirable in the show ring.
- Lift the dog from the sink, wrap him in a warm towel and gently pat the excess water from the coat.

Drying

- After towel-drying, use a hair dryer to finish the process. Use a medium or low setting, and keep it a good 10 inches (25 cm) from the dog, to avoid scorching his skin.
- Dry in the direction of the coat growth, brushing while you do so. Remember, this is different from most breeds – the Pom should be brushed/stroked/dried from the bottom of the back toward the head.
- When drying the dog's tummy, get him to lie on his side – it will make your job a lot easier.

Trimming

This is the part that fills new owners with dread! The best advice is to ask the breeder to show you how it should be done. Perhaps ask if they can supervise you for your first few trims, too. Eventually, however, you will have to go it alone. This is the best way to learn.

It's only through practice and experience that you will become accomplished. Yes, you may make a few mistakes along the way, but as long as you learn from them, there's no harm done.

- When he's thoroughly dry, brush the coat again, as described on page 55.
- Lay your Pom on his side and cut any long hair between the pads.
- Now trim around the edges of the foot, to give a neat, cat-like appearance (see page 60).
- Next, turn your attention to your dog's ears. Hold the ear leather in your hand, and carefully trim the ears close to the edge to neaten them and to enhance their small appearance.
- Assess the body hair next – trim any long, stray hairs (including the front feathering on the legs), always remembering that you are trying to achieve an overall round appearance. However, do not get too carried away – the Pom should not appear sculpted like a Poodle. Any trimming should be done subtly, leaving the dog looking quite natural. Just remember, you cannot replace what you have cut off, so go easily and carefully.

REGULAR CARE

Brushing

Every day, the coat should be given a quick brushing to remove any tangles before they develop into mats. Do not go overboard – a thorough daily brush may remove all the undercoat. Pay particular attention to the rear end, which can become soiled, and to the armpits and the base of the ears, which are prone to knots and mats.

If you are exhibiting in the show ring, you may need to tidy up your Pom with a little judicious trimming.

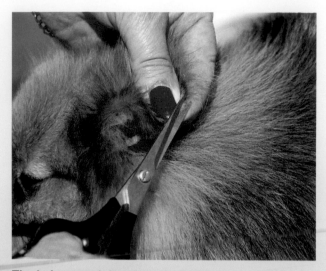

The hair around the ears can be trimmed to give a better shape.

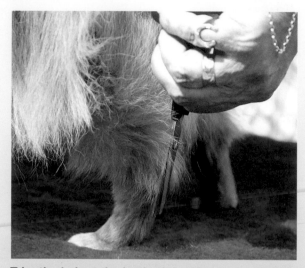

Trim the hair at the back of the hind legs and tidy the front feathering.

For reasons of hygiene, trim the hair around the anus.

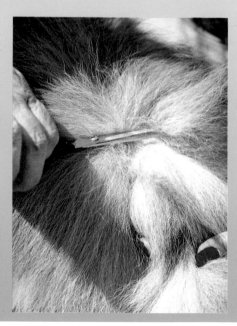

Trim at the base of the tail to allow the tail to lie flat on the back.

Eyes

The Pom's eyes tend to be a little watery. If they are not cleaned every day, a buildup can collect in the corner of the eye, leading to infection because the fluid cannot drain away freely.

Use two cotton pads, one for each eye, to avoid cross-contamination.

Dampen the pad in boiled water that has cooled and gently wipe around the eye, particularly in the corners.

Ears

Poms are prone to ear mites, which cause a great deal of discomfort to the dog. Clean the ears weekly, using a moist cotton pad. Do not clean deep inside or use cotton swabs that could damage the inner ear.

Consult your veterinarian if the ears are red, have a buildup of wax or dirt, or if your Pomeranian keeps scratching at them, because he may need ear medication.

Teeth

In common with other Toy breeds, the Pomeranian is prone to dental problems. Rotten teeth and infected gums are painful to the dog, cause difficulty eating, often require sedation for proper care, may require the removal of some or all of the teeth, and are costly to treat. All in all, poor dental health is best avoided!

The best way is by brushing the teeth daily. Some people laugh at such a concept, but a dog is not designed to eat modern commercial foods – ripping up a carcass in the wild would remove plaque naturally, but this is not something most Pomeranians do nowadays!

Use a small child's toothbrush (or a small dog one), and buy some canine toothpaste (do not use toothpaste intended for human use).

Canine toothpastes are available from pet supply stores in several flavors, including a meat variety! Brush the teeth as you would your own, and give your Pom a treat afterwards so he learns to look forward to his daily dental care – a game with his favorite toy, a good cuddle, or half a carrot should do the trick!

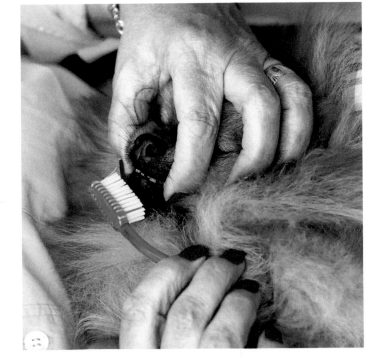

The teeth should be cleaned regularly.

Nails

Check your dog's nails regularly to see if they should be clipped. If they are overly long, you will hear them tapping against a hard floor, and will see that they detract from the neat, catlike appearance of the foot. If they are long, they will need clipping.

Poms should have dark nails, which makes nail clipping a little bit more difficult. In the middle of the nail is the quick – the nerves and blood supply. In some light coat colors, it can be seen as a dark line running lengthwise down the nail, but, since most Poms have black nails, it is impossible to see. Cutting into the quick is very painful to the dog and causes bleeding, so great care must be taken.

- Lay your Pom on his side.
- Hold one of the feet gently but securely in one hand, and, with the other, clip a small amount from the end of the nail – just the tip.
- Do this for all the nails on the foot, if necessary.
- Inspect the foot. Are the nails short enough now, or do they need a little more shaved off each one? It is better to snip a little and have to snip a little more than to take off too much and cut into the quick.
- Don't forget the dewclaws (the nails that are high up on the foot) – they are removed in most puppies, but not all.
- Make sure you have something to stop the bleeding should you accidentally nick the quick. Pet supply stores sell a range of products to apply to the cut. In a pinch, cornstarch will do.

Trim the nails if they grow too long.

If you are at all unsure about the procedure, ask your dog's breeder, groomer, or veterinarian to show you what to do. When it comes to your beloved Pom, it is better to be safe than sorry.

General checks

Every day, run your hands over your dog's body to check for any lumps, bumps, or anything out of the ordinary. Assess his general condition, and report anything that concerns you to the veterinarian. Many diseases and disorders can be treated effectively if caught early.

The final result – groomed to perfection.

RESCUED DOGS

In the U.K. there is not a huge rescue problem among Pomeranians. The Pom is quite a minority breed. With so few dogs around, breeders screen prospective owners very carefully and can afford to be very choosy about whom they sell to. And, with such small litters, there are often long waiting lists. The whole process is very slow and drawn out. Impulse buyers soon lose patience or are filtered out by breeders.

In the United States, however, there are many Pomeranians in need of rescue. This is because the breed is numerically much larger than in the U.K.

Most dogs end up in rescue through no fault of their own. Divorce (and the subsequent changes to someone's living and working arrangements) is a chief cause.

Health problems mean that some owners are no longer able to care for their pets. Reluctantly, a number of Poms are put into rescue when their elderly owner goes into a nursing home or dies.

Although they are utterly devoted to their owners, Poms can be rehomed successfully. After a settling-in period (ranging from a few days to a few weeks, depending on the individual dog), they seem to take to their new lives with vigor.

KISSES FOR KIZZY

Patricia Thorne from Staffordshire, England, has had Poms since the age of seven. Now, nearly 50 years later, Pomeranians are still the love of her life – so much so that she simply cannot bear the thought of one needing a home. If she hears of a Pom in such a predicament, he doesn't remain homeless for long!

"When I was seven, my father said I could have any dog I wanted. I went through a book featuring different breeds and found the Pomeranian. It was quite a difficult breed to get hold of in those days, but my mind was set, and I eventually got Cuddles.

"Cuddles was nearly 17 when she died, and her daughter, Sally, also lived for more than 16 years. I married and had children, a cat for my daughter, and numerous birds, hamsters, and rabbits, but I always wanted another Pomeranian. After the death of Smudge, my daughter's cat, she suggested finding a Pom puppy, and so Ari arrived to join our family.

"My first rescued dog was Scrappy, who was around 12 years old when I got him. His elderly owner could no longer look after him, and I took him on.

HEALTH PROBLEMS

"Scrappy had a very strong, unpleasant smell, and was shaking so badly that it took about 30 minutes cuddled inside my jacket before the shaking stopped. We bathed him and the only time we ever noticed the smell was when we were out and he saw me walking away from him.

"He had a lot of health problems. His teeth were very bad and had to be removed, and he had a severe heart murmur. He would suddenly yelp loudly and then keel over, losing consciousness and control of his bladder.

"I nearly lost Scrappy in the first two months of having him, but managed to get his strength up and nurtured him back to health. But he was never a well dog, and I lost him about 16 months later.

Scrappy: a loving dog, with a marvelous character.

"I was heartbroken when he died. He was such a loving dog, with a marvelous character. Unlike most Poms who have foxy faces, he had quite a round, squishy nose, and was gorgeous. Because he had needed so much care, I was utterly lost when Scrappy died – I had so much time on my hands – so I contacted the breed rescue organization again.

"It was then that I heard about Kizzy. She's six years old, and I've had her for 18 months. Kizzy was in rescue because her elderly owner had died.

On arrival, Kizzy was very submissive and would cower or roll over on her back and lick madly. She now rushes to me and runs around like a whirling dervish when she greets me. Like Scrappy, Kizzy isn't playful and didn't much like going for walks (she does now) – I can only think that their previous owners couldn't exercise them. Interestingly, they also wouldn't go up my stairs – the previous elderly owners must have lived in apartments.

STARTING FROM SCRATCH

"Kizzy settled in very quickly. She was quiet for awhile, but it wasn't long before she was barking at noises and wandering around the house on her own. My other dog, Ari (short for Aristotle), really took to Kizzy (he had ignored Scrappy completely!).

"The only problem we had was with housetraining. Kizzy doesn't ask to go outside, she just goes wherever she is. I don't think she was trained properly before, so we have to start from scratch and treat her as if she is a puppy. We take her outside a lot, and have to watch her very carefully for any warning signs.

"The downside to taking on a rescued dog is that you usually don't know their history. For example, Kizzy is quite terrified of my sister, but we don't know why. My sister loves Poms (Scrappy loved her, and Ari adores her), but Kizzy goes to pieces when she sees her – and even defecates from fear. She must be reminded of someone in her past.

"But the advantages to rescuing a Pom are numerous. Kizzy is very affectionate. Although she doesn't play, she does cuddle! The moment you sit down, she's on your knee. I think she would have been a great companion to her former owner – sitting on her lap, giving love all day, every day.

"I love Poms – the look of them, their characters, each one an individual, everything about them. They just look like real dogs – tiny wolves. They are so cuddly, yet intelligent, alert, and energetic. Everything you want from a dog in a small package."

Kizzy: an affectionate Pom who loves her cuddles.

A sudden change of circumstances can mean that a Pom has to lose his home.

Matching the right home to the dog is the key to successful rehoming. If the dog shared his home with an older person and led a quiet, peaceful life, he will not take well to family life, with other pets and children. Thankfully, breed rescue organizations are thorough in their work, and very few – if any – dogs are returned once rehomed.

OLDER DOGS

Like most Toy breeds, the Pomeranian has a good life span, many living well into their teens. Most remain as perky and lively as when they were puppies, but some slowing down is inevitable.

The senses are likely to deteriorate – the dog's eyesight will worsen and he may eventually become completely blind. His sense of smell and taste will not be so sharp, and his hearing may also be affected. The sparkle of youth will dim a little: The coat may not be quite so lustrous and healthy looking, the dog may need more naps, and he may refuse to go outside in cold or wet weather. At heart, however, he is likely to remain as fun-loving, affectionate, and alert as ever. However, you shouldn't ignore the fact that your Pom is getting older. You don't need to turn your life upside down to accommodate him, just make some basic changes to your routine and lifestyle to ensure that his changing needs are met.

- Older Poms like their routines. If you are going away and cannot take your Pom with you, it is better to arrange for someone to come and look after him than it is to put him in a kennel.

- Do not move your furniture around. If his eyesight is failing, he will bump into the rearranged furniture. Even blind dogs manage to navigate perfectly through rooms – provided everything is kept where it was. That said, Poms are fast little learners – they rarely bump into the same thing twice!

- Toy breeds are notoriously fussy eaters, and the Pom is no exception. This is likely to get worse as your Pom gets older, because his failing sense of smell and taste will mean food is not that appetizing. You may have to opt for smellier flavors or heat the food a little to release its aroma.

- If your oldie has bad teeth (or becomes entirely toothless), he may have difficulty eating a dry, complete food (some have no difficulty, however!). If he is having problems, either switch to a meat diet, or add water to the dried food so that it is easier to chew and swallow. Warm water will also help to make the food smellier (see above).

- Weight can be a problem. Some Poms gain weight because they may be exercising less; others cannot keep the weight on. Weigh your dog weekly (see page 52), and consult your veterinarian if there are significant changes. If the weight loss is due to old age, increase the number of meals – your Pom may find it easier to eat four small meals a day rather than one or two larger ones.

- A checkup every six months is a must for older dogs. Many disorders can be treated, but early detection is vital. Weekly home checks should also be continued (see page 57).

As your Pom starts to age, he will need special consideration.

- Your Pom is likely to revel more in his home comforts. If the weather is intemperate, he may not want to go out, preferring to doze on a warm, soft lap, or in front of a fire. Play it all by ear. If it's blowing a gale outside or is wet, then obviously don't force him out for a walk. In better weather, though, it is important that he is kept moving and mentally stimulated, so encourage him to have a sniff around the yard or a walk around the block.

- Incontinence can become a problem. Sometimes, a medical condition can be responsible (such as cystitis), so consult your veterinarian. If there is no obvious health cause, it may be that your Pom just can't be bothered to go outside (see Chapter Six: Problem Solving).

- Make sure your Pom is given plenty of opportunities for cat-naps throughout the day. Like puppies, oldies need lots of sleep, so give him somewhere quiet to retire to, where he can rest undisturbed.

Morris Hutchinson from Darlington, England, has owned Pomeranians for 24 years, and finds they always save the best for last…

"I have had many Poms over the years, and they have all been a pleasure to own.

"I only have one at the moment, Mandy. She is a 15-year-old sable, whom I hand-reared when she was a puppy. Her mother wouldn't feed her, so I had to do it. Her aunt was a Champion, and I thought Mandy might take to showing. I have shown my dogs, making two Champions, but I decided the time had come to just enjoy the company of the Poms – they had become older and even more loving.

"Poms do not age until late in life. Maybe at around 13 or 14 years they go a little misty-eyed and their hearing starts to deteriorate. Otherwise, they usually remain fit and healthy until the end.

"Mandy is deaf and has no teeth, so we have to soak her food in water. But she still goes for daily walks, and is as playful and loving as ever. In fact, Poms often become even more affectionate as they age.

"Poms don't much like change. If their sight is impaired, the furniture in the home shouldn't be moved around. Provided everything stays where it is, even totally blind dogs cope remarkably well, and can find their way around the home and yard with ease.

ATTENTION

"Mandy's mother (Katie) died last year at the age of 16 and a half, and, for the first time, Mandy was the only dog in the house. Being the youngest, she was lowest in the pack and would always allow the other dogs to eat first. She was completely lost when she was the only one left.

"Around this time, she started to come to bed with us at night. She still sleeps at the foot of the bed – it is as if she doesn't want to be downstairs, alone. She seeks out attention from us when she needs a cuddle, and enjoys being on our laps.

"Mandy has become so loving and endearing. As they get to know you more and more, Poms become especially affectionate. They are just a pleasure to own."

Katie (left) who lived to be 16, pictured with her daughter, Mandy.

SAYING GOODBYE

After years of being a faithful, loving companion to you, the time will eventually come when you will have to part with your beloved Pomeranian. Some Poms die of old age in their sleep, some drop down dead without warning, but you should also be prepared for having to make some difficult decisions.

As a caring pet owner, it is your responsibility to ensure that your dog does not suffer. If your Pom has an illness or injury from which he will not recover, and he has a poor quality of life, then it is your duty to ensure he dies with dignity. Opting to have your pet euthanized is never an easy decision, but you will know in your heart of hearts whether it is the right one.

Although it is a difficult choice to make, do not keep your pet alive for your own sake. It is better to let him die peacefully than to linger in pain.

Euthanasia is performed by a veterinarian – either in the veterinary clinic or in your own home – and involves injecting sedatives intravenously so that the dog falls into a deep sleep and his heart eventually stops. It is painless for the animal, and, although it will be considerably more painful for you, it is important to stay with him during the procedure, if you can bear it. After years of giving you love and friendship, the least you can do for your Pom is to be with him when he dies.

You may decide to take the body home with you – to bury in the yard or at a pet cemetery,

In time you will be able to look back on the happy times you spent together.

A DOG IN A MILLION

Hazel Woodfine from Devon, England, has had Poms for most of her life. A successful breeder and exhibitor, Hazel has shared her home with many, many dogs, but one stands out above all the rest – Brandy.

"Brandy was one of a litter of two. He didn't seem anything special, at first – show-wise – but I took him to some small shows and he did well. We moved up from there, and eventually ended up competing in Championship shows.

"At the first big show we went to – the Royal Cornwall Show – Brandy won his puppy class, then Best of Breed, then Best Toy! We were then meant to compete for Best in Show, but the weather was atrocious – even the tents were blowing away – so we didn't attend.

"From there, Brandy's show career went from strength to strength, and he soon became a Champion (see Chapter Nine).

"As an experienced breeder, I've sometimes lived with 20 Poms at a time, and Brandy was one of the best dogs I've ever had. He was a show-stopper – he had lovely movement and a fabulous coat; he was regal, and, when he walked into the ring, he seemed to say, 'Look at me, here I come.' Around the house, he was a gentleman. He had a lovely character – he was always full of life, and very affectionate.

"I knew something was wrong when we drove to a show and he was sick in the car. Brandy had traveled all over the country and had never been ill before. When we arrived at the show, he wouldn't walk on the lead. He kept twisting his head, so we retired from the ring.

Tragically, Brandy had to be put to sleep when he was only four years old.

When we got home, he had his first seizure. He had a brain tumor.

"It was a terrible shock – Brandy was only four years old. He was put on medication to help control the seizures, but there was nothing else that could be done. Within three months, he really started to deteriorate. He started to hold his head to one side, stopped eating (and had to be fed with a dropper), and was eventually walking in circles.

"I just couldn't see him like that – he was usually so fit and regal. I took him to the veterinarian to be euthanized when the time came, but I was so upset, I couldn't stay. My husband was with Brandy, but I just couldn't do it. I regret not being there for him.

"Losing Brandy broke my heart. I never showed another dog again after he died. Out of all the dogs I've ever had, he was the apple of my eye.

"Although I was heartbroken, and regret not being with him when he was put to sleep, I have no regrets about my decision to end his suffering. You must always consider your dog, not yourself, and put them first. It is so sad to do, because you love them so much, but you must do the best for your dog. To do anything else would be selfish."

or to have a personal cremation. There are many urns and caskets to choose from, if you wish to keep the ashes, or you may decide to scatter them in the yard or along his favorite walk.

Alternatively, your veterinarian can arrange to have the body cremated. If you want the dog's ashes returned to you, ask for a personal cremation, otherwise the body will be incinerated with other pets too.

If you have never owned a pet before, do not be surprised by the grief you feel after losing your Pom. He is a special member of your family, and it is only natural to feel devastated when he is no longer there. How long it takes to come to terms with the loss depends on the individual – it can take weeks, months, or even longer.

Some people cope best by throwing themselves into dog ownership once more, and getting another Pom soon after. Others cannot cope with having another dog for awhile, believing it is a betrayal to their former dog's memory. It may help to choose a different color or sex of dog, but getting another of the same breed is the greatest tribute you can pay to your Pom. As the playwright Eugene O'Neill said, when writing the last will and testament of his Dalmatian, Blemie, "There is nothing of value I have to bequeath except my love and my faith. These I leave to my master and mistress, who I know will mourn me most. Now I would ask her, for love of me, to have another. It would be a poor tribute to my memory never to have a dog again."

CHAPTER SIX

PROBLEM SOLVING

Poms may be small, with angelic little faces, but they can be demons at times! It is rare for any dog owner, of whatever breed, to go the full length of a pet's life without any training or behavior problems, and you may encounter an occasional difficulty with your Pom at some point. Early training and socialization are essential for preventing most problems, but you may have to overcome a hurdle or two later in your dog's life, too. Here are some of the more common difficulties in the breed.

YAPPING

Poms are great communicators. Treated as one of the family, they enjoy being talked to, and especially enjoy talking back! It should come as no surprise that the Pom likes the sound of his own voice – Toy breeds are renowned for this trait, as are spitz breeds, so it is definitely in the Pom's blood.

Of course, barking *per se* is not a problem. It is the dog's only way of communicating the approach of a stranger, pain, anger, boredom, and a gamut of different emotions. Problems arise when the dog starts barking to tell you that a leaf has just blown across the lawn or that there is a fly in the kitchen, or when the dog's "off button" simply doesn't seem to work!

The Pom is alert to everything that is going on – he must learn that he does not always need to vocalize his feelings!

First, address the reasons why your dog keeps barking. Is he bored? Can he see a neighbor's dog? Often, dealing with such problems (i.e., by making sure the dog is mentally stimulated or by changing your fencing) is enough to moderate the barking.

In some cases, though, if the barking has been left unchecked, it becomes habitual. This involves some time and patience in consistently retraining your Pom:

- When your dog barks inappropriately (e.g., more than the occasional warning bark), tell him "Quiet!" firmly. Do not shout or scream this command, because this will only excite him further – if you raise the volume, so will he!

- Be consistent. Do not tell him "Quiet" one day and overlook inappropriate barking the next because you are too tired or can't be bothered. This will give mixed signals to the dog and will undermine the value of the command.

- If your dog is barking for a valid reason – because the mail has arrived or because a visitor has entered the house – let him bark a little (assuming that you want a warning bark whenever anyone approaches the house), then tell him "Quiet." This should teach him that endless barking is not necessary.

- Another method is to distract him from barking. Ideally, this can be done when you can predict the times that your Pom barks. For example, if you know that your Pom always yaps when the mail is delivered, then, a few minutes before, take your dog to a back room, away from the front door, and

If your Pom has a toy in his mouth, he cannot bark at the same time.

play a game with his favorite toy. With time, this will break the habit of his morning mail bark. Then it is a case of commanding "Quiet!" if he barks again, to ensure he does not slip back into his old ways.

- A successful way to silence your dog is to give him a favorite toy to hold in his mouth. A dog cannot do this and bark at the same time!

TOP TIP

Poms are worse in stereo! If you have more than one dog, they will set each other off with their barking, so train them individually. Keep them separate at times when they are more likely to bark (e.g., if visitors come), and only allow them back together again once each one responds to "Quiet!"

Noiseless fun

Dogs enjoy barking. The key is to make being quiet even more fun and rewarding.

- When your dog responds to the "Quiet" command, give him a treat and praise.
- However, don't fall into the trap of being trained by your dog. Some are canny enough to realize that barking is rewarding, because it is followed by "Quiet" and then a treat!
- If you find your dog is deliberately barking to get a treat, use another training method described in this section.

Introducing distractions

When your Pom's barking can reliably be controlled on command, it's time to introduce distractions. This is where his self-control is really tested.

- Arm yourself with some of his favorite treats and toys, and get his attention by giving him a treat or playing a game with him.
- Give him a tiny taste of a treat intermittently, and, when he is totally focused on you, introduce whatever stimulus it is that makes him bark (e.g., ask a friend to walk a dog past the door/window).
- You will really have to fight for his attention now – say his name in an excited way, wiggle the toy a little more, praise profusely, and provide a regular supply of treats.
- Initially, the stimulus should only be introduced for a short time (15 seconds or so).
- Lavish praise on your dog and reward him handsomely if he doesn't bark. If he does, tell him "Quiet" and reward if he complies.
- When he ignores short distractions, gradually increase the length of time he is exposed to them.

INCONTINENCE

In common with many Toy breeds, Poms seem to be prone to lapses in housetraining, where they forget their early puppy lessons and relieve themselves indoors. This is quite different from territorial urine marking (see page 74). Perhaps because of this Toy reputation, owners often put up with it – rather than putting an immediate stop to such inappropriate behavior.

If you find that your adult Pom starts using the house as a toilet, retrain him at once as if he were a puppy (see page 39). Take him outside very regularly (every couple of hours), and praise him well when he performs on command.

FAIR-WEATHER DOGS

Assess the times that your dog toilets indoors. Does it only occur in wet or cold weather? Many Toy breeds, even thick-coated ones that descend from Arctic breeds, hate inclement weather. If you suspect that this is the reason for your dog's incontinence, then reassess his toileting routine. Is there a covered porch that you can take him to in wet weather? If not, perhaps accompany him outside and hold an umbrella over him. Or perhaps put a cat litter box by the back door and encourage him to use it. Think dog!

If he persistently eliminates on a particular area, it is likely that the scent of past accidents is attracting him back. Even if you clean the area with general household cleaners, it only masks the smell to humans. Dogs have very sensitive noses and will be able to detect what the deodorizer is meant to be hiding. In fact, some cleaners actually attract dogs and encourage them to be incontinent, because they contain ammonia!

- Wet the area with warm water, and work an enzymatic cleaner into it, to create a lather. Rinse thoroughly with warm water, making sure you remove all trace of suds.

If house-training breaks down, you will need to go back to basics and become extra-vigilant.

- Consider also barring your dog's access to his favored site. Perhaps keep the door to that room closed, or move a piece of furniture over the spot, so he can't reach his improvised toilet area.

- Above all, be extra-vigilant. Watch the dog closely for any warning signs that he needs to relieve himself. If he sniffs the ground and circles, take him outside immediately.

Lifting a leg

If your Pom lifts his leg against furniture, tell him "No!" firmly. Clean the area thoroughly and perhaps spray it with a commercial scent deterrent or a vinegar and water solution to discourage him.

To stop the behavior (which is quite different from incontinence), it is important to investigate the reason why he is doing it. Is there another male dog in the house with whom he feels the need to compete? Does he feel insecure? Does it happen after visiting dogs have been in "his" house?

Leg-lifting is notoriously difficult to stop, so ask the advice of your veterinarian. Overactive hormones are unlikely to be the sole cause of the behavior, so neutering by itself will not always stop the problem. However, your veterinarian can refer you to a reputable pet behaviorist, who can design a remedial program specifically for your dog.

FUSSY EATING

This is another area where the smart Pom trains his owner! The breed is not generally known for having a hearty appetite (though there are always exceptions). If owners find that their dog is not eating enthusiastically, most people panic and immediately offer something tastier. This, the dog will quickly devour. However, he soon learns that if he abstains, the stakes are raised and the menu offered to him becomes far more appetizing.

Some dogs just will not eat, no matter what. If your dog is otherwise healthy, put his food down as normal, and remove it after 10 minutes if it is uneaten. Many dogs will learn that refusal doesn't mean something tastier comes along – only that they are left hungry.

Encourage your Pom to eat, but do not allow him to become a fussy eater.

If a dog refuses to eat for more than 24 hours, you should consult your veterinarian to check that nothing is physically wrong. If your dog is given a clean bill of health, it may be worth discussing whether the veterinarian can recommend any appetite stimulants.

Where a Pom is perfectly healthy but utterly stubborn, he will refuse meal after meal after meal, to the point of endangering his own health. In such extreme cases, you have no other option than to give in. Perhaps mash a small amount of something tasty (and smelly!) into his normal food to stimulate his appetite (e.g., cooked chicken meat or fish – with bones removed). Such dogs are unlikely to eat two large meals daily, so feed small, frequent meals throughout the day to ensure they get sufficient nourishment.

SPAY AND NEUTER

If you do not plan to breed or exhibit your Pom (see Chapter Nine), you may want to consider the option of neutering. Many owners use it to forestall the development of problem behavior as their dog reaches adolescence. However, you should bear in mind that this will help only if hormones are directly responsible for the undesired behavior – for example, if the male dog is aggressive toward others because of excess testosterone, or if he is mounting cushions as he becomes sexually mature. Most behavioral problems are caused by inadequate socialization and training, and neutering will not help.

Health benefits

Behavioral problems aside, you should consider neutering before your dog reaches adolescence because there are important health benefits. When a male dog is castrated, his chances of developing prostate disorders in later life are significantly reduced, and incidences of testicular cancer become nonexistent. When a female is spayed – which involves removal of the womb – she has a much lower risk of developing mammary tumors and she will never be in danger from pyometra, a life threatening infection of the uterus.

Convenience

The convenience of having your Pomeranian neutered or spayed should not be underestimated. Pomeranian females will begin their first heat season at about six to nine months of age, with seasons occurring every six months thereafter. If your female is not spayed, you will have to cope with the bloody discharge she produces (it can get everywhere) and you will also have to keep her indoors for several weeks.

While a female is in heat, she will attract the attention of all male dogs in the surrounding area. Do not underestimate your Pom's intelligence – little she may be, but she will be surprisingly devious in her attempts to escape the house to mate with one of many more-than-willing partners. Some owners find themselves faced with the problem of a pregnant female despite their precautions and vigilance. If this happens to you, you will have to pay for all the subsequent veterinary costs, not to mention the expense and time of rearing a litter and finding homes for all the puppies.

It is not only owners of female Poms who may find neutering convenient; dog owners may be surprised at the benefits. A male Pom becomes sexually mature at about eight months of age, and, if your dog is unneutered, he will pick up the scent of any female in heat in his neighborhood. During this time, your dog will be prone to wandering – and look out if you accidentally leave your gate open or if your Pom slips his lead when out walking. Your dog will make a beeline for the female, desperately attempting to get close enough to mate with her. No amount of tasty treats or cuddles from you will compare to the mating urge!

Castration will also reduce your Pom's chances of developing unsociable behavior such as scent-marking, mounting, and aggression.

Possible problems

There are some possible problems associated with neutering, the most common complaint being weight gain. However, this is not necessarily the case. Neutered animals are less active (they are not wandering the streets seeking potential mates), which is why they are prone to putting on weight. If you adopt a sensible diet and exercise regime (see Chapter Five), there is no reason your Pomeranian should gain weight.

Some owners of females have reported incontinence after spaying. However, this is very rare, and the majority of owners will never encounter this problem.

Your veterinarian will help you to decide whether neutering is a good idea.

Another disadvantage is that the coat of a neutered Pom is different from the coat of an intact animal. It is often more profuse, woolier than normal, and therefore more difficult to groom.

Surgical risks

Neuturing and spaying are surgical procedures, which should be carried out only by a qualified veterinarian. As with any surgery, there is an element of risk, but neutering is carried out so often today that it is generally considered to be a routine operation. The risks from surgery are actually very small. It is up to you to discuss the matter with your own veterinarian.

Making the decision

The decision to neuter will depend on a number of factors, such as your lifestyle and whether or not you plan to show your Pom or simply to keep him as a pet. You will need to weigh up the pros and cons carefully and then make your decision.

Some veterinarians claim it is important to neuter before the dog reaches sexual maturity; others strongly believe it should take place after the dog has developed fully. If you decide to have your Pom neutered, make an arrangement to talk to your veterinarian about his own views, and about what is best for your individual Pom.

CHAPTER SEVEN

THE VERSATILE POMERANIAN

The Pomeranian is a breed that is happiest when kept busy. Although the average Pom is more than content to laze away the hours sitting on his owner's lap, reveling in cuddles and adoration, he will soon become bored if this is all his life consists of. It should not be forgotten that, while the Pomeranian is a Toy breed and

The Canine Good Citizen program is designed to train dogs to achieve basic obedience and (good) manners.

primarily a companion, he is descended from working spitz-type dogs and he has lost none of the quick intelligence possessed by his ancestors.

CANINE GOOD CITIZEN

Like any breed of dog, the Pomeranian should be taught good manners and how to behave appropriately in a variety of everyday situations. Never make the mistake of letting your beloved pet become an overindulged lap dog with no sense of how to behave around people and other dogs.

The Canine Good Citizen program is an excellent way to improve on your Pom's initial training and socialization. In the U.K. the program is known as the Good Citizen Dog Scheme, and is run by the British Kennel Club. The American Kennel Club (AKC) equivalent is the Canine Good Citizen program. Both programs aim to encourage responsible dog ownership through education and training.

To receive his Canine Good Citizen certificate, your Pomeranian will need to:

- Accept handling and grooming
- Respond to basic obedience commands
- Meet another dog in a friendly manner
- Walk on a loose lead in a controlled way
- Walk confidently through a crowd of people
- Accept being approached and petted by a stranger

Provided you trained and socialized your Pom as a puppy, he should not find any of these tests too difficult. You can also enroll in one of the many Canine Good Citizen training clubs in Britain and the United States. To find out more, contact your national kennel club.

OBEDIENCE

Poms are a lot smarter than many people give them credit for. Their glamorous appearance blinds many dog lovers to the fact that this is a breed that possesses intelligence in the same abundance as good looks. Given the right training, Poms are easily capable of performing well in competitive Obedience.

Obedience is a fun sport that can be enjoyed by any breed and at any level. For Pomeranians, the most important requirement is that you make the sport fun. If you approach training in too regimented a way, with little variation and inadequate rewards, your Pom will become bored and lose interest.

Pomeranians are not difficult to train, but training any dog for Obedience competition requires a great deal of commitment and patience. If you are a highly competitive person who likes to be the best and to win often,

consider another breed for Obedience. However, if winning is not the be-all and end-all for you, and you think you would enjoy training and competing – as well as the obvious advantages of having an extremely well-behaved dog – then Obedience could be just the thing for you and your Pom.

Your national kennel club will be able to provide you with details of clubs in your area.

AGILITY

Agility can be enjoyed by people at all levels, from those wishing to simply have fun, to people who take part in national competitions. It is enormous fun for dog and handler alike, and it is a great way of keeping your dog (and yourself!) very fit.

The sport is best described as an obstacle course for dogs. Each dog must successfully negotiate a series of obstacles, within a set time and with no faults. The winner is the dog that has the fastest time with the least mistakes. The obstacles include:

- Hurdles: which the dog must jump over.
- The long or broad jump: a series of elements laid on the field, which the dog must clear in one jump.
- Tunnels and chutes: of which there are two types – the solid tunnel (an open tunnel, similar to a pipe) and the collapsible tunnel (which has an open entrance and a cloth tunnel that the dog must push his way through).
- Weave poles: a series of upright poles fixed in the ground and set in a line. The dog must weave in and out of the line of poles.

Julie Howard, from Kokomo, Indiana, sadly lost her much-loved Pomeranian, Beau, in July 2002, but not before he made a lasting impression in the world of Obedience…

"I got Beau from his breeder when he was still a puppy. His full kennel name was Exmoor's Mr. Beau-Regard, CD, but I've always called him Beau, for short. I started Beau at puppy kindergarten when he was four months, and we began formal Obedience training shortly after that.

"It was quite easy for me to get started. My local kennel club held classes at the same location as the puppy kindergarten, and I knew several of the instructors. I jumped at the chance of enrolling because I thought it would really help Beau's socialization. When I first had him, he had a bad habit of screaming whenever a stranger wanted to hold him or pet him, and I was anxious to overcome this problem.

"The first class we attended, we did no Obedience training whatsoever. Beau was simply passed around all the people in the class until he stopped screaming. Only then did the instructor allow him to come back to me. Beau quickly realized that no one was going to hurt him and that he would only receive attention from me when he was quiet and well-behaved. After this experience, Beau was fine, and he would let anyone touch him and pet him.

"Obedience training is good fun but it requires quite a serious level of commitment. Depending on the dog and the level you want to reach, you can train several evenings a week. I found that training worked best when Beau and I learned an exercise in class, and then practiced at home for the week before the next class. Practice, patience, and dedication are the key elements.

"Beau loved to please me, and this really helped when teaching him Obedience exercises. Like all Poms, he was incredibly smart and picked up things very quickly. He loved the one-on-one attention he received from me, although food came a close second. Beau was very food-motivated and a good supply of treats went a long way toward enlisting his cooperation.

"Beau achieved his title when he was three years old. I'll never forget one competition when he got first place. I remember the judge calling number 20 for first place. Although I knew my number, I had to check my armband, look at Beau, and listen to my friends and instructors cheering wildly before I realized that we had won first place. We beat 22 other dogs and it was one of the proudest moments of my life.

"I miss Beau terribly. After he retired from Obedience competition, he was a much-loved, very pampered pet, adored by me and my parents. At the moment, I am not competing in Obedience myself, although a couple of dogs I have bred are competing with some success. I would advise anyone interested in the sport to give it a try. It is a wonderful way for you and your dog to bond and to spend time together."

The proud moment when Beau took first place in an Obedience competition.

- Seesaw: which the dog must run up, balance in the middle until the seesaw tips, and then run down the other half.
- Dog walk: a narrow, elevated walkway that the dog must cross.
- A-frame: a steep, A-shaped ramp that the dog must run up and down.
- Tire jump: a tire suspended in a frame, which the dog must jump through.
- Pause table: A table that the dog must jump onto and remain still upon for a set period of time (usually about five to ten seconds).

Agility competitions are divided into classes for different sizes of dogs, with Pomeranians competing in the smallest class. In this class, the obstacles are slightly smaller in size, to make it easier for your Pom to jump the hurdles, etc. Furthermore, your Pom will not have to compete against the larger breeds, so it is more than possible that, with dedication, you and your Pom could be very successful.

Agility is a fairly demanding physical activity, for dog and handler alike. Consequently, you will need to ensure that you and your dog are fit and healthy before you take up the sport. For the same reason, the kennel clubs in most countries refuse to allow puppies or growing dogs to compete, because the demanding nature of some of the obstacles can damage growing joints. Your national kennel club will tell you about age restrictions in your country, and provide you with information about Agility training clubs.

LEARNING TO LEAP WITH LADYBUG

Dizzy Dollies Pondside Ladybug is a four-year-old Agility dog belonging to Roberta Malott of Pondside Toys in Blenheim, Ontario.

"Several years ago, my friends and I founded the K-9 Thunder Paws Agility Group. We were looking for ways to have fun with our dogs and Agility seemed like the perfect answer. There were no Agility clubs in our area, so, once we knew what we were doing, we offered classes, built some equipment, and began to host trials. At the time, I had a Yorkie who had some aggression problems, but by giving her a fun job to do on the Agility course, she learned to concentrate on things other than her aggression. My Pom, Ladybug, arrived when she was just six weeks old, but my other dogs had enjoyed Agility so much, I knew I would introduce Ladybug to it as soon as she was old enough.

"Ladybug took to the sport straight away. She loves to have fun and she adores treats, so when you combine the two, you have a very happy little dog! I use clicker training, supplemented by lots of treats, and it is a system that works really well for Ladybug.

"It is important to start off slowly in Agility. No dog should train for jumping obstacles until they are older than 18 months, but there is a lot of training you can do before this age, without damaging a young dog's joints. Tunnels and chutes, weave poles and any of the ground obstacles are fine for a young dog to tackle. I

**Ladybug flies over the hurdles.
(Photo courtesy of Kevin Potvin.)**

also started Ladybug practicing the dog walk, but by laying a plank on the ground and getting her to walk along it, as opposed to using an elevated walkway that she could fall from.

"It is also important to take things slowly because you run the risk of losing your dog's interest if you push too hard. The dog has to learn to trust you and he won't if you ask him to do something he can't cope with. Fortunately, Poms are very people-oriented and they love to have fun. As long as they are in good physical condition and they are trained correctly, most Poms take to the sport very well indeed.

"Ladybug learned how to tackle all the obstacles very quickly, although we need to practice increasing her speed. Above all, she simply enjoys being out there and having fun. I have only had one problem with her, and that

was due to her coat. Agility trials are normally held in the summer months and Ladybug is very heavily coated. During one trial, she became so hot that she left the course and picked a nice, cool, shady spot under the official's chair. It was an unconventional finish, but I decided it was better for her to quit than it was for me to push for a finish if she really felt that hot.

"I have big ambitions for Ladybug and I would love to see her win some titles. However, having fun is the most important part of the sport, and I am extremely proud when Ladybug simply completes the entire course with me. I have also started working with another Pom, and I am sure he will do well, too.

"I'd advise anyone interested in the sport to try it, but I would remind them that the dog's welfare comes first – Agility should be safe and rewarding for the dog, and, above all, it should be fun for both the dog and the handler."

A confident run through the tunnel.

ON YOUR MARCO!

Kim and John Cagle from Houston, Texas, regularly compete in Flyball with their four-year-old Pomeranian, Prince Marco Polo.

"We saw a Pom running Flyball at a dog show in Houston, and the owner told us about the smaller balls and lower jumps for little dogs. Marco loved to play ball at home, and he had already tried Agility, so we thought he would enjoy Flyball. Another consideration was that dogs are allowed to bark in Flyball, which Marco likes to do!

"It took a few weeks to find a club that practiced in our area. Initially, we joined a small, newly forming team, which meant that Marco received lots of training. It was fairly easy to teach him to go over the jumps, as he has a tremendous ball drive and he already knew the command "Over" from his Agility training. One problem we did encounter was getting Marco to return to us over the jumps. He had a tendency to prance around, showing everyone that he had caught the ball. His trainer, Terrie O'Connor,

Kim Cagle, pictured with Prince Marco Polo.

FLYBALL

Flyball originated in the United States just over 15 years ago. Since that time, the sport has become increasingly popular on both sides of the Atlantic. It can be basically described as a canine relay race with hurdles. Two teams of four dogs compete against each other on two identical tracks (each track is 51 feet or 15.5 meters long), and the winning team is the team that finishes first.

Each dog runs along a track, jumping over four hurdles on the way. At the end of the track is a Flyball box. The dog has to trigger the box to release a ball, catch the ball in his mouth, and then return to the start of the track, again jumping the hurdles on his return journey.

When the first dog returns, the second dog is released to run the course. This continues until all the dogs have run. If a ball is dropped, or if a hurdle is missed or knocked down, the dog must run the course again after the last member of the team has run.

Because Pomeranians are small dogs, there are a number of adaptations needed. For example, you may find it necessary to replace the standard-size tennis ball with a smaller version. Many clubs now provide smaller Flyball boxes especially for small breeds. These boxes require less physical force to trigger the ball-release mechanism. To find out details of your nearest suitable club, contact your national kennel club.

called it his "victory lap." He seems to have gotten over that, though.

"Probably the longest bit of training we had to do was to teach Marco to trigger the Flyball box. Marco is larger than many Poms, weighing about 9 pounds (4 kg) and measuring 11 inches (28 cm) at the withers, but, because he is so small, he had to learn how to jump on the box at full speed. Smaller Poms may have trouble triggering the box and clearing 8-inch (20-cm) jumps. Fortunately, once Marco learned the technique, he never looked back.

"Although we received lots of valuable training in our initial club, Marco didn't get to compete, so, eventually, we left to join a larger club, the Flat Out Flyers. After 17 months of training, we entered Marco in his first tournament. His performance that day is one of my proudest moments – he earned 25 points and his Flyball Dog title. Within a few more tournaments, he achieved his Flyball Dog Champion title. At a recent tournament in Memphis, he ran heat after heat and race after race flawlessly, all in front of the crowd. He has also raced several six-second runs – a phenomenal time – during tournaments.

"I am looking forward to many more years of Flyball racing, and I hope to see Marco rise higher in the Pomeranian Flyball rankings. Racing against another Pom, as we have done in one tournament, is great fun.

"You have to be careful with Poms, making sure their joints are up to the stress, and it can take a long time for them to learn what to do, but they are bright, eager little dogs and the wait is well worth it. There may not be many Poms running in Flyball at the moment, but those that are racing make great competitors. Marco will look at the dog in the other lane and try to overtake him. Some people may scoff at the idea of the cute, fluffy Pom doing Flyball, but I would tell them to come and watch my Pom race!"

After patient training, Marco has become a top-class Flyball competitor.

FREESTYLE

Canine Freestyle developed out of Obedience. Traditional Obedience exercises, and other fancy moves, are set to music in a choreographed sequence, with dog and handler as dancing partners. It is becoming increasingly popular as a dog sport, and, since its inception a few years ago, it has incorporated many new moves.

Today's performances are often highly elaborate and flamboyant.

There are numerous organizations involved with Freestyle, each with their own competition rules. However, generally, most performances last less than five minutes, and judging is divided into two areas:

BAD, BAD LEROY BROWN

Peggy Shambaugh, from Ohio, got interested in Freestyle four years ago, at the age of 75. Peggy's current dancing partner is a three-year-old Pom named Buddy, which just goes to show that Freestyle can be enjoyed by people and dogs of all ages!

"I used to go to dog shows with a friend of mine, Paula, and, it was at one of these shows, about four years ago, that I first found out about Freestyle. I was fascinated and I began reading and watching everything I could find on the sport. I called Patie Ventre, then of the World Freestyle Canine Organization, and I watched some excellent videos by Sandra Davies. Not long afterward, I began a training club, with other like-minded enthusiasts, and I've been involved in the sport ever since.

"Shortly after my interest in Freestyle began, I acquired Buddy. I've always been a lover of big dogs before now, but I had sound reasons for choosing a Pom. Freestyle demonstrations mean I travel over the country, and I hate to put a dog in the cargo hold of an airplane. A small dog can stay with you on the journey, which is much more pleasant for me and for the dog. I chose a Pom because I had one when I was a small child and when I was in high school. I knew it was a breed I could get along with.

"I've had Buddy since he was eight weeks old, and I began training him immediately. Small dogs can sometimes be a bit yappy, so the first thing I taught Buddy was to inhibit his barking instinct. Then we began Freestyle training. The first move I teach all my dogs is the spin, which Buddy learned very quickly.

"Buddy adores Freestyle – it means he gets lots of attention, although his main reason for cooperating is the food! I think our favorite routine is *Bad, Bad Leroy Brown,* written, recorded, and made famous by Jim Croce. It's a brilliant performance – a real crowd pleaser.

"Today, Buddy and I give demonstrations all over the country, at schools, at nursing homes, and at dog shows. That's one of the wonderful things about Freestyle; it appeals to people of all ages and all backgrounds, not just dog lovers. I've also found that it can help to overcome behavioral problems in dogs. I've been on the board of directors of the Humane Society for many years, and I suggested Freestyle training at one of our training centers. Freestyle is based on Obedience, although Freestyle moves appear less formal and more enjoyable to learn than traditional Obedience exercises. I thought teaching some of our dogs how to dance might help them to be more obedient, and, therefore, more likely to be rehomed with success – we get many dogs returned to us because their behavior is a problem. Since we introduced the idea, we have had a 50 percent success rate, which is a big improvement and one we are very pleased with. It just goes to show that Freestyle is a sport that anyone – human or canine – can take up and enjoy."

Musical partners: Peg Shambaugh and Beau James (Buddy).

- **Technical:** This assesses accuracy, the synchronization between dog and owner, and the degree of difficulty in the routine.
- **Presentation:** This covers costume and the artistic flair shown in the choreography.

Freestyle is very enjoyable to watch, and even more enjoyable to perform. It is also a great way to get fit.

However, it requires a great deal of training. You will need to have an extremely strong rapport with your Pomeranian and he will need to be trained to a fairly high standard of Obedience before you can take up the sport.

If your dog is well behaved, obedient, and willing to learn new things, you have already laid the foundations for Freestyle training - everything else you can learn.

Contact your national kennel club for more information on Freestyle organizations and how to get involved.

CHAPTER EIGHT

A SPECIAL BOND

Pomeranians are descended from much larger, sled-hauling, spitz-type dogs. While they are diminutive in size, Poms have retained many of the characteristics of their larger cousins. They are highly intelligent, active and vivacious dogs, and they should be given the opportunity to fulfill their potential through further training.

For many people, the appeal of the Pomeranian lies in the breed's affectionate, light-hearted disposition. This is, of course, one of the reasons why the Pom is so highly regarded as a companion dog. However, it is a mistake to assume that these qualities cannot be extended to a wider range of activities. There are several working avenues that really make the most of the Pom's sweet-tempered, extroverted nature.

There are a number of Poms working as hearing dogs and therapy dogs. These roles make the most of the Pom's personality, and the breed's small size is an advantage rather than a hindrance. Dogs for deaf people are specially chosen as puppies, undergoing a lengthy training period before their working life begins. Consequently, you won't be able to train your Pom in this field. However, if this sort of work appeals to you, and you think your Pomeranian would enjoy the experience, there is nothing to prevent you from becoming involved with therapy work, bringing joy to those who would otherwise have no contact with animals.

SERVICE DOGS

There are many types of servicce dogs, working with a variety of people – from the blind and the deaf to those who are disabled or handicapped. The dog's role is to fill the gaps created by the owner's disability, whether that is barking to alert a deaf owner that the doorbell has just rung, or helping a handicapped person to put on their socks. Worldwide, there are few Poms working as dogs for the disabled, because the breed's small size restricts the help they can give their owner. However, in recent years, Poms have really come into their own as hearing dogs for the deaf.

Hearing dogs

Poms love nothing more than lots of cuddles and plenty of attention, and hearing dogs develop an extremely strong bond with their owners. Shape and size are irrelevant when it comes to recruiting hearing dogs. The main requirement is a quick, alert personality, which the Pomeranian possesses in abundance. As the examples on the next few pages show, Poms can make a real difference to a deaf person's quality of life.

GETTING TO KNOW GEORGE

Lynn Currie, from Larkhall in Scotland, is the proud owner of hearing dog George, a beautiful red Pomeranian who acts as Lynn's ears.

Lynn Currie has grown in confidence since working with George.

"I have been profoundly deaf since I was born, but it was not until the year 2002 that I got a hearing dog through Hearing Dogs for Deaf People. I had never owned a dog before, and, because of my lifestyle, I asked for a small dog. George was a rescue dog, found wandering as a stray in Wales. I was sent a photo of him and fell in love instantly. I couldn't wait to start my training with him. To begin with, he had to be assessed and socialized, but, after that, it was all systems go at the training center in York.

"George was taught how to respond to certain sounds, such as the smoke alarm, the telephone, and the doorbell. It was a steep learning curve for me too, as I had to learn how to recognize which sound he was alerting me to, and how to respond in the appropriate way so that I didn't confuse him.

"Once I got George home and began sharing my day-to-day life with him, I couldn't believe the difference he made. My day begins with George waking me. He is so small, I have to place a stool next to the bed so that he can jump up to wake me in the mornings! One day, I overslept. Thinking George had failed to wake me, I told him off, only to discover that my alarm clock was faulty. I had to spend a long time making up to George for that. He, of course, loved every minute of being spoiled rotten for a day. Needless to say, I now own a new alarm clock.

"Once George is satisfied he's woken me, his next task is to listen for the mailman. Breakfast is often quite amusing, because, if I burn the toast, George lets me know that I've set off the smoke alarm!

THERAPY DOGS

Therapy dogs perform an invaluable service to a wide range of people, and Poms make ideal therapy dogs. The breed possesses a natural curiosity about life – most Poms love to meet new people, reveling in the attention that their adorable appearance seems to inspire. Using positive, reward-based methods, Poms are easy to train and they are naturally cheerful and friendly.

As the proud owner of a Pom, you already know the joy that owning this little ball of fur can provide. A rambling walk on a sunny day, long cuddles on the sofa, the bond created through the intimacy of grooming, your dog's unconditional love – it is often easy to forget just how much our dogs enrich our lives. Imagine if all this was taken away from you…

Sadly, this is the case for far too many people. Many of the people visited by therapy dogs are lifelong animal lovers who greatly miss the companionship provided by their pets now that they are no longer able to keep them. Even more people have never experienced the joys of pet ownership.

Therapy dogs visit a variety of establishments, including residential homes, schools in deprived areas, hospitals and hospices, and prisons. People in these institutions benefit greatly from regular contact with a therapy dog, and these visits can go some way toward conquering people's feelings of isolation and loneliness. Furthermore, research has shown that regular contact with pets helps people physically, as well as mentally. Recently, there has been a lot of media coverage about how contact with pets can boost our immune system, and how children brought up with a family dog are less susceptible to allergies and ailments such as the common cold.

Therapy programs are becoming increasingly popular in Britain and the United States, but they rely on an army of volunteers and their pets. Sadly, there are not enough to go around, and

"George has enabled me to live life in a way I'd never have dreamed possible before. I can enjoy my garden now, because George will alert me if the telephone rings. When I'm out, George is an attention-grabber – complete strangers come up to pet him and they talk to me about him. It's wonderful to be so involved in daily life again, and my confidence has grown enormously.

"As well as all the practical things that he does for me, George is a wonderful companion. He's great company – affectionate and amusing – and he keeps me occupied while my husband is out at work and my daughter, Lynsey, is at school.

George loves Lynsey. Whenever she arrives home from school, he gets so excited that he races around the room. His favorite pastime is removing Lynsey's socks from her feet. For some reason, no toy has the same appeal as Lynsey's socks.

"George is the best thing that has ever happened to me (with the exception of my husband and daughter). I can go anywhere with him and do anything. He is a lovely, happy dog. He is full of affection and likes nothing more than to lick me to death. I wouldn't be without him, and I'd advise anyone else suffering from hearing loss to find out more about hearing dogs."

LISTENING TO MIKEY

Lona Jennings, from Washington State, has suffered progressive hearing loss over the last 45 years. Here she describes the difference her hearing dog, 11-year-old Pomeranian Mikey, has had on her quality of life.

"I have had a progressive hearing impairment since I was a child. In some ways, losing my hearing at such a young age has helped – I've gotten used to it. However, losing some of your ability to hear has a profound impact on everyday things, such as listening for the doorbell or the telephone, and it is to little things like this that owning a hearing dog makes all the difference.

Mikey has made a huge difference to his owner, Lona Jennings, and in return she ensures he is rewarded with love, attention, and exercise.

"Acquiring a hearing dog is a lengthy process, as the organization needs to be sure that they are matching the right dog with the right owner. After all, it's no good sending an active Labrador to act as a hearing dog for a housebound, elderly person. I was interviewed and evaluated by someone from Dogs for the Deaf, and it was decided that Mikey would be the perfect hearing companion for me.

"When I was a child, my family owned a Pomeranian/Pekingese cross, whom I adored. When I was allocated Mikey by Dogs for the Deaf, I was delighted to discover that he was a Pomeranian, as I was familiar with the breed already. You don't get to choose the breed you like, but I couldn't have chosen better myself!

"Once I had Mikey, I had to learn how to recognize what he was telling me. I also had to learn basic obedience commands with him, as well as a fair bit of dog psychology. It all helps you to form a bond with your dog. Mikey acts as a sort of canine go-between for me and the rest of the world. He fills in the gaps that my hearing loss has created.

"When I am out, Mikey is a great conversation starter. He is a non-standard black-and-tan Pomeranian, and I am frequently asked, 'What kind of dog is that?' The other favorite line is, 'What a cute little dog!' Fortunately, Mikey's presence reminds strangers that I am hard of hearing, and they speak more clearly and more slowly to me, which is a great help. Sometimes, I feel like I'm living with a celebrity, and I definitely don't feel as isolated as I did. When you are hard of hearing, there is a wall of silence that separates you from the rest of the world. Mikey encourages us all to break through that wall.

"Owning a hearing dog has had a huge impact on my life, and I wouldn't be without Mikey. However, I'd advise anyone thinking of applying for a hearing dog to remember that your dog is a dog first and foremost. Yes, he will alert you to sounds and be an invaluable hearing aid for you, but you must never lose sight of the fact that he is a dog and a companion. He should be treated like an equal partner, and, in return for his helping you, you must remember to give him plenty of attention, love, and exercise."

CACTUS AND SILVER BUCK

Mary Evans and her husband, Glyn, from Gloucester in the U.K., regularly visited hospitals with her two Pomeranians, Cactus and Silver Buck.

"It all started with our Rottweiler, Suzi. She had such a beautiful temperament that we were asked to register her as a Pets As Therapy (PAT) dog. After that, we used to take the Rottweiler and our Pomeranians on visits.

"Cactus and Silver Buck adored therapy work. We used to visit a local 'cottage' hospital, where most of the patients were long-term residents. The effect the dogs had was quite incredible. You could see people's faces light up when we arrived. Patients that were a little intimidated by the Rottie's size would have no hesitation in trying to get a cuddle from a Pomeranian, so we really were able to help everyone.

"It's easy to see what the dogs get from therapy work – endless cuddles, and lots of biscuits and treats! However, therapy work has a great effect on the patients, and not just for the short time they are with the dogs. Our visits had such a profound effect on the patients that the hospital governors established a policy of encouraging visitors to bring in their pets.

"At one point, the hospital had a husband and wife in at the same time. They were cat owners, but they really enjoyed visits from Cactus and Silver Buck. The visits seemed to accelerate their recovery, to such an extent that the hospital staff eventually asked the couple if they would like to have their own cat stay with them at the hospital. They, of course, jumped at the chance, and a mere four months later – a lot sooner than anyone expected – husband and wife were well enough to leave the hospital and go home! It just goes to show how contact with animals is so beneficial it can actually improve your health.

"One of the most rewarding experiences we had with Cactus and Silver Buck was visiting patients who had been paralyzed in some way. People tend to assume that paralyzed patients are unable to feel any sensation in their affected limbs. That's simply not true. Poms are small enough to sit on a frail person's lap, and that's what ours did. Then, we would pick up the patient's hand and run it slowly over the dog's coat, so that the patient was 'stroking' the dog. When we did this, you could see the patient's eyes light up. It was very moving.

"Sadly, Cactus and Silver Buck have passed away, and, due to changes in Glyn's work schedule, we are no longer able to make hospital visits with our dogs. However, I'd advise anyone who owns a dog with the right temperament to have a go. The satisfaction you get is enormous; the patients love it and the dogs are delighted by all the attention and treats. Everyone wins!"

Cactus and Silver Buck: ambassadors for the Pomeranian through their therapy work.

Much-loved Pomeranian, Poppy, was a regular visitor to homes for the elderly, bringing a lot of joy to the residents' lives. Poppy's owner, Marian Kelsall, describes the world of the therapy dog.

"Poppy was my first Pomeranian. Prior to that, I kept German Shepherd Dogs, but since owning Poppy, I have fallen in love with Poms.

"I used to be a dog trainer and professional handler in the 1960s and 1970s, but then I had an accident that prevented me from carrying on. I had a very severe back injury that kept me off my feet for two and a half years. I still suffer pain today, if I overdo things. During my recovery, I found out about the Pets As Therapy (PAT) scheme. Having been a trainer in the past, it was relatively easy for me to get started in therapy work, despite the stringent tests each dog has to pass – does the dog have an excellent level of basic obedience? Is he good with people? Does he have a laid-back temperament? All my dogs more than meet these criteria, and so I began visiting with my German Shepherds.

"I visited residential homes for the elderly, and I enjoyed the work immensely. My German Shepherds had such an impact on the residents' lives that I decided to try visiting with a Pomeranian. Poppy was a huge success. She adored all the attention and couldn't get enough.

The residents loved having a little dog to make a fuss of, and the big advantage Poppy had over my GSDs was that she was small enough to sit on people's laps to be fussed over. Poppy was an extremely glamorous dog, with the sort of face that people fell in love with instantly. The only problem I ever had when visiting with her was that people refused to let her go! I had a very hard time trying to leave after a visiting session.

"Sadly, Poppy died in a flood, along with five other dogs of mine. It broke my heart and Poppy was sorely missed by the residents. For awhile, I was unable to visit the homes, because everyone kept asking for her. It was a difficult time. However, I am now working with another beautiful Pom, Champers. Therapy work is so worthwhile, and it spreads a great deal of happiness. I'd advise anyone thinking of becoming involved to go right ahead, and Poms are great at the job."

Poppy: a welcome visitor for elderly residents.

demand is very high. If you decide to get involved with your Pom in therapy work, you will have the added satisfaction of knowing that you are helping to provide a much-needed service. However, you cannot simply show up at an establishment with your dog. It is essential that your Pom is assessed beforehand, to make sure his temperament and training are suited to the work. To become a therapy dog, your Pom will need to be evaluated by one of the therapy dog organizations in your country. All therapy dogs must be totally trustworthy, and comfortable in unfamiliar surroundings and the company of strangers. This is why the Canine Good Citizen program (see page 79) is so important. To find out more, contact your national kennel club for details about therapy dog organizations, or try searching the Internet.

EDUCATING YOUNG PEOPLE

It is a sad fact that cruelty to animals seems to be on the increase, and we have all seen horrific cases reported in the media. However, there is a small army of volunteers dedicated to reversing this trend.

In some countries, national programs have been established to educate children about the responsibilities of dog ownership and how to approach dogs in the right fashion. In those countries where no national program exists, there are a number of local organizations fulfilling the same role. If this work appeals to you, asking your national kennel club, or searching the Internet, should provide you with details about programs in your country.

Mostly, handlers take their dogs to schools, where children can be educated informally in a comfortable and familiar environment, and where the handler can ensure that no harm comes to the dog.

It is hoped that, over time, these programs will result in a new generation of people who are comfortable around dogs, and who will be responsible owners should they have their own dogs in the future.

CHAPTER NINE

SEEKING PERFECTION

For many centuries, people have owned and loved Pomeranians. Although the breed has been miniaturized over this time, the Pom still retains many of the same features from when, even further back, he was a sledding, guarding, and hunting dog in Northern Europe (see Chapter One).

To ensure that the Pom does not lose his unique characteristics over time, breeders and judges work to a breed standard. This is a written blueprint that describes the ideal dog of each breed. All aspects are covered – from his size and coat, to his personality and foot shape. Breeders are then able to use suitable dogs in their breeding program, to ensure that these standards are maintained, and, in the show ring, judges can select dogs that most closely conform to the ideal dog.

THE BREED STANDARD

Each national kennel club is responsible for its own breed standards. There are inevitably some differences between countries, but, essentially, they are all fairly similar.

Here is a summary and explanation of the key points of the British and American standards. For further details, contact your national kennel club for a copy of the standard that specifically applies in your country.

General appearance

A compact, cobby (short-backed) Toy dog that is alert, active, and intelligent.

Characteristics

Sound, good-tempered, happy-go-lucky, and animated.

Temperament

Outgoing, intelligent, and lively.

Head and skull

The Pomeranian has a foxy face. The skull should be slightly rounded but not domed. The muzzle

The Pomeranian should appear compact and dainty.

Mouth

The Pom should have a scissors bite, meaning his top teeth closely overlap his bottom ones.

Neck

In keeping with the dog's short, square overall appearance, the neck is short and set well into the shoulder.

Forequarters

The forelegs are straight and in proportion to the size of the rest of the dog's body. The dewclaws are generally removed at a few days old.

is fine, but not snipey, and there is a distinct stop (indentation between the eyes where the nose meets the skull).

Eyes

The bright, dark eyes have a keen, intelligent expression. They are medium-sized, and should not be too wide apart. They should be slightly oval (almond-shaped). The British standard requires black pigmentation around the eye rims for white, orange, shaded sable, and cream dogs. Others are self-colored (i.e., beaver has beaver-colored pigmentation). The American standard requires black in all but brown, beaver, and blue dogs, where pigmentation is lighter.

Ears

The small, erect ears are set high on the head, fairly well apart but not excessively so.

The typical foxy face of a Pomeranian.

The Pom's coat is his crowning glory.

Body

The back is short, and the body is quite rounded. The chest is fairly deep (but not wide), and this aspect is emphasized by the breed's characteristic mane-like frill.

Hindquarters

The hind legs are fine-boned, with moderate angulation, and should be perpendicular to the ground and parallel with each other from the hock to the heel. A few strains produce dewclaws on the hindlegs.

Feet

The Pom has round, small, catlike feet, and stands well up on his toes.

Tail

The tail is set high, and curls over the back, where it lies flat along the spine. The Pom has a fox-like brush the tail-coat is profuse, with long hair that is harsh to the touch.

Gait/movement

The Pom's movement is smooth and free. He moves briskly and buoyantly.

Coat

This is the Pom's crowning glory. As would be expected of a spitz breed that originated in the cold, hostile environment of Iceland and Lapland, he has an insulating double coat. The undercoat is soft, thick, fluffy, and short. It is covered with the long, straight, harsh guard hairs of the topcoat that protect the undercoat from getting wet. The coat is abundant around the neck, chest, and front part of the shoulders, producing a profuse, impressive frill or mane.

Color

In Britain, most colors are permissible. Acceptable solid colors are:

- Beaver (gray-brown)
- Black
- Blue (pale)
- Brown (brown with an orange hue – all shades acceptable)
- Cream
- Orange (bright)
- White (must have no lemon or other color in the coat).

A few white hairs are acceptable but not desirable in these colors, and white or tan markings are frowned upon.

In addition to solid colors, the following are also acceptable:

- Parti-color (even patches of color on the body – the dog should not have a tan or white chest or feet)
- Sable (another word for black, and any color can have sable mixed in – for example, orange sable, or wolf (cream) sable). These are classed as solid colors provided there is no patching
- Shaded sable (shaded evenly with three or more colors).

All the coat types compete together. Where all else is equal, preference is given to solid-colored dogs.

In the United States, however, Open Classes at specialty shows may be divided by coat color:

- Red, orange, cream, and sable
- Black, brown, and blue
- Any other color, pattern, or variation.

In the United States, all colors and patterns are permitted:

- Any solid color
- Any solid color with lighter or darker shading of that color
- Any color with sable or black shading
- Parti-color (white with any other color distributed in patches; a white blaze on the head is preferred)
- Brindle (the base color is gold, red, or orange-brindled with strong black cross-stripes)
- Black and tan (black with tan or rust markings clearly defined over each eye, on the muzzle, throat, and forechest, on all the legs and feet, and below the tail)

Size

In the U.K., the ideal weight for dogs is: 1.8–2 kg (4–4.5 lb); bitches: 2–2.5 kg (4.5–5.5 lb). This is fairly unusual in the dog world – in most breeds, males are larger. In the United States, Poms can be between 3 and 7 pounds (1.3–3.1 kg), but the ideal weight is 4 to 6 pounds (1.8–2.5 kg).

SHOWING

As the proud owner of a Pomeranian, you probably think that your dog is the most beautiful in the world. However, dog shows are not beauty contests; they are entirely about improving the breed. By recognizing the dogs that most closely conform to the breed standard, it is hoped that these dogs will be bred, and so will pass on their desirable traits to the next generation.

Finding the right dog

If you want to show your dog seriously and not just at fun shows, you will need to make sure that you have a good example of the breed. Most breeders will not sell show-quality puppies to the pet market unless the would-be owners have expressed an interest in showing, so most people acquire a new dog specifically for showing. That said, your dog should be an adored pet first and a show dog second.

Handling

At handling classes you will learn how to exhibit your dog to his best advantage. Handling classes are a great exercise in socialization and obedience as well as preparing you and your Pom for the show ring. Your national kennel club will be able to provide you with details of training clubs in your area, and classes will also be listed on the Internet and in the dog press.

Types of shows

There are several types of dog shows, ranging from local fun shows to prestigious Championship shows, such as Crufts in the U.K. and Westminster in the United States. Most categorize the dogs according to Group. In the U.K. and the U.S., the Pomeranian is placed in the Toy Group.

Showing is a highly competitive business, and you need to be confident that your dog has the quality to make the grade.

U.K. Shows

There are a number of informal shows held throughout the country by various organizations, but the main shows are known as Limited, Open, or Championship shows.

Limited shows: Often, these can be entered only by members of the organization hosting the show. Usually, different breeds within the same group (e.g., all the breeds in the Toy Group) compete against each other in so-called "any variety" classes, though there are also shows just for Poms.

Open shows: As the name suggests, these are open to all. Open shows often contain breed classes as well as "any variety" classes.

Championship shows: These are the biggest and most important shows. For each breed, there are usually two Challenge Certificates (CCs/tickets) available, one for the best bitch and one for the best dog. At the end of all the classes, the winners are entered into a final class (known as "the challenge") to compete for the ticket. Any male or female that wins three CCs under three different judges becomes a Show Champion. Sometimes, there may be no specific classes for Pomeranians, but the show secretary will be able to answer any questions about which class you should enter.

U.S. Shows

Like the U.K., there are a number of informal or match shows held, but to make your dog a Champion, you need to compete in a licensed or point show, where Championship points are offered. There are two types of licensed shows:

Specialty shows: Specific breeds of dog, or group of breeds, compete in these shows (e.g., Pomeranians only, or several different Toy breeds).

All-breed shows: These are similar to Championship shows in the U.K., with breeds divided into classes and winners chosen from each class. The winners of each breed are entered into a Group competition, and the winners from the Group competitions are entered into a final contest to win Best in Show. The maximum number of points a dog can earn in any one show is five, and Champions are made by earning a total of 15 points. The 15 points need to include two majors (three-, four-, or five-point awards), awarded by different judges.

Your first show

Before entering your first show, it is a good idea to attend some shows as a spectator. This will give you some idea of what to expect when you are ready to compete with your own dog. You will gain a clear understanding of the standard you can expect to find yourself competing against, and you will witness how the more experienced handlers show their dogs.

When you feel you and your Pomeranian are ready to begin competing, check the dog press for details of forthcoming shows. You will need to send off for a schedule, which will be sent to you along with an entry form. Your handling instructor will help you fill in the form correctly.

If you are unfamiliar with the world of dog shows, you should try entering match shows to begin with. These will give you valuable experience before you try the larger, more competitive shows.

Success and failure

There are always exceptions, and the dog press is full of examples of novices who have taken the show world by storm, but at your first show it is unlikely that you will do particularly well. Do not let this dishearten you. Your dog's performance and your handling skills will improve with experience, thereby improving your result. Always remember, however, that you should love your Pom unconditionally – it is not his fault if he falls a little short of the expected standard. You should love him unreservedly, however he performs – you always take the best dog home.

SUE, SCOUT, AND DEENA TOO...

Sue Sanderson from Malvern, England, began showing Pomeranians almost by accident, after falling in love with her friend's dogs.

"I knew a little about showing before I began exhibiting Pomeranians. My daughter was actively involved in junior handling before she became a teenager, and I have several friends who are professional breeders and exhibitors. I had tried exhibiting another breed, but it was not until I watched a friend showing her Poms that I knew I had to own one of these spirited and flashy dogs.

"My first Pomeranian was called Kirk. We started off at fun shows and gradually progressed to Open shows and the like. He did fairly well in the show ring, achieving enough to earn his stud-book number. Sadly, however, he suffered a small stroke and was withdrawn from the show ring.

"Now, I show two delightful Poms – Warleggen Suburban Fox Among Sandchize (otherwise known as Scout) and Warleggen Ring Out the Auld Among Sandchize (Deena). They are brother and sister through the same Champion sire, although their mothers are different. Deena has won a Reserve Challenge Certificate and Best Bitch, and I'm really proud of her. However, I think I'll have more success with Scout. He is only two years old at the moment, but he is very much an up-and-coming dog and I have high hopes for him – he has already gained his stud-book number.

"When Scout was a puppy, I entered a Championship show with two friends. We were all exhibiting puppies from the same litter – four in all. Although it was their first Championship show, all four qualified for Crufts, coming 1st and 2nd in Minor Puppy Dog and 1st and 2nd in Minor Puppy Bitch – a record in the breed! That said, however, no matter how well Scout or Deena perform in the show ring, they are both the most beautiful dogs in the world, in my opinion.

"I love showing my Poms and they love being in the show ring. My two are quite extroverted in nature, and love nothing more than to strut their stuff for the judge. In fact, Poms are an ideal breed for the novice show person because they love the show-ring environment. Of course, you will always find some dogs that hate it, but you will quickly tell if your dog is enjoying the experience by the way he behaves. A really important part of showing that novices will need to learn, however, is the art of trimming. Presentation goes a long way in the show ring.

"Every time I exhibit, I learn a little more about the breed, and about the world of showing, although I have a lot left to discover. It is a favorite joke among Pom enthusiasts that you are a novice in the breed until you have been showing them for more than 20 years, and I'm still very much in the early days of my apprenticeship!"

Sue Sanderson has a word with Deena (Warleggen Ring Out the Auld Among Sandchize) while they are competing in the ring.

Win or lose, you know you are taking the best dog home with you.

BREEDING

All purebred dogs registered with a national kennel club have a pedigree. This is a record of the dog's family history, showing his parents, grandparents, and so on. From this, you will be able to see if any famous dogs feature in your dog's ancestry, and also what type of breeding was used to produce him.

Inbreeding

This is seldom used in the breed any more. It involves mating close family members – e.g., father to daughter or mother to son. It is traditionally used to get results very quickly (instead of patiently waiting four or five generations to achieve what you want). Sounds ideal, doesn't it? It isn't. Inbreeding really should be left to the experts – and often

they won't use it either. The reason? As well as accentuating the good points, inbreeding also intensifies the bad. Without incredibly careful planning, and good luck, badly deformed puppies can result. Steady progress is best made through line breeding or outcrossing.

Line breeding

This involves breeding more distant relations – those from the same family, but not immediate relatives. It works to consolidate and reinforce family traits, and to retain a line's characteristics, so is the preferred method of breeding. To stop the line becoming stale, occasionally new blood is then introduced (outcrossing, below).

Outcrossing

This is where two completely unrelated dogs are mated. It can be a hit-or-miss affair, as it can be difficult to predict the results of using two different lines. However, with an expert eye, detailed knowledge of the dogs' family history, and a degree of luck, outstanding dogs can be produced. Because it can be unpredictable, it is often used in conjunction with line breeding – to introduce certain qualities into a line and then to breed the dog to the kennel line to ensure that the family traits are not lost.

The following pedigrees feature show Pomeranian Champions that illustrate line breeding and outcrossing in action.

LINE BREEDING

Ch. Cradarr Military Tattoo.

Bred and owned by Eric and Pauline
Wallace, Koko is a good example of line
breeding, with Cradarr dogs on both sides
of his pedigree.

He has won 16 Challenge Certificates,
three Toy Groups at Championship shows,
and the Pomeranian Contest of
Champions. Other wins include Best of
Breed at Crufts in 1997 (the same year that
he was crowned top Pomeranian), gaining
the same honor in 1999, and Best Veteran
at Crufts 2002. At the 2002 Northern
Pomeranian Show, he won Best Veteran,
Best Dog, and Best in Show. He has sired
four Champions to date, together with
several winners of Challenge Certificates.

Ch. Cradarr Military Tattoo
Photo: Russell Fine Art

Parents	Grandparents	Great-Grandparents	Great-Great-Grandparents
Cradarr Military Man	Linak Apache	Ch. Toybox Platignum Phantom	Toybox Small Print
			Silver Slipper of Toybox
		Linak Amour	Pomlyn Puss-in-Boots
			Linak Andromeda
	Cradarr Fascination	Ch. Toybox Platignum Phantom	Toybox Small Print
			Silver Slipper of Toybox
		Dandave Mighty Tasty	Ch. Gaytroll Mighty Mouse
			Black Elegance
Cradarr Fanfare of Cabana	Cradarr Choir Boy	Ch. Cradarr Drummer Boy	Dandave Mr Dreamaker
			Cradarr Sugar and Spice
		Pomlyn Shady Lady	Pomlyn Puss-in-Boots
			Gold Charm of Majada
	Ebony Lady	Dandave Mr Dreamaker	Ch. Majada Sunny Boy at Katula
			Majada Sweet Surrender
		La Golandrina	Dandave Tar Baby
			Longtowns Black April

OUTCROSSING
Ch. Lireva's Shooting Star.
Ziggy, as he was known to his friends, was one of two pups in a litter. His parents (who are entirely unrelated) had produced very good Poms in the past, but with Ziggy, they really hit the jackpot! He won 17 Challenge Certificates at Championship shows, all but one with Best of Breed. From these, he won eight Toy Groups and four Reserve Toy Groups (at a time when there were only two placings in the groups). He won two Bests in Show, and two Reserve Bests in Show. His most prestigious win was Reserve Supreme Championship at Crufts 1984. He was Top Toy in the U.K. in 1983.

Ch. Lireva's Shooting Star

Parents	Grandparents	Great-Grandparents	Great-Great-Grandparents
Pippitty Bo of Lireva	Toymarsh Sir Winston	Flash of Aurum	Impudence of Aurum
			Twilight of Aurum
		Toymarsh Honeypuff	Windyhulls Saucy Dinky
			White Snowy of Windyhulls
	Andersley Madam Rochas	Andersley Draytonvilles Dinky Dandy	Ch. Cynpegs Little Extra
			Draytonvilles Rosebud
		Andersley Pendy Dare Madam	Int. Ch. Andersley Dazzler of Hadleigh
			Andersley Asuki
Montravia Golden Star	Hadleigh Honeystar	Ch. Hadleigh Starlight	Ch. Modelstar of Hadleigh
			Hadleigh Zoira of Zanow
		Hadleigh Honeysweet	Hadleigh Golden Beam
			Hadleigh Honey Love
	Golden Charm	Sable Dandimite	Covington Golden Boy
			Gilmoss Honeybunch
		Canberra Golden Tina	Ch. Golden Legend of Aurum
			Canberra Golden

PUPPY TO CHAMPION

Ch. Thelbern Mardi Gras: British breed recordholder,
with 39 Challenge Certificates

Show Pomeranians all develop in different ways – some are born show-stoppers and remain so until they retire from the ring. Others are born with great potential, but never live up to their early promise; and others do not initially seem anything special, but surprise their owners by a last-minute transformation!

As these photos show, there are many phases of a dog's development from puppy to Champion.

Mardi pictured as a ten-week-old puppy.

Heading for maturity at nine months and winning her first Reserve CC.

The promise is fulfilled at three years of age.

Ch. Thelbern Mardi Gras: Breed recordholder with 39 Challenge Certificates and Toy Group winner at four years old.

CHAPTER TEN

HEALTH CARE

Although the Pomeranian is classified as a Toy breed, this lively, intelligent extrovert is by no means just a lap dog. He is the smallest of the spitz-type of dogs, which are considered to be the most ancient canines known to man. The breed has been established in England for well over 100 years and about 70 years in America.

The Pom's working background serves him in good stead – this is a healthy breed, relatively free from breed-specific conditions, with the possible exception of occasional kneecap problems (see page 126).

However, first we must begin with the important subject of preventative care. This involves more than just ensuring that your pet is regularly vaccinated and wormed.

PREVENTATIVE CARE

Responsible preventative care involves:
- **An adequate vaccination program.**
- **Comprehensive parasite control.**

- **Adequate exercise.** Poms are active dogs that need controlled daily exercise or they can quickly turn into couch potatoes. Obese Pomeranians are an all-too-familiar sight in urban veterinary practices (see page 51). However, do not overexercise young animals – it can result in joint and bone abnormalities.

- **Grooming.** One of the great attractions of this delightful breed is the abundant stand-off coat, giving the Pom the appearance of a ball of fluff. This double coat consists of a dense undercoat covered by the long, straight, harsh topcoat. Regular attention is required to keep the well-groomed appearance. Grooming does not only involve brushing and combing, but also attention to ears, eyes, teeth, etc., to avoid major problems in the future. Along with many other Toy breeds, the Pom does have dental problems, many of which can be avoided by home dental care (see page 59).

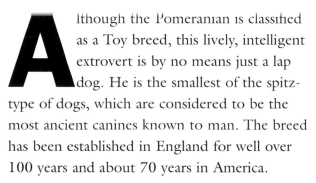

- **Training.** Pomeranians are alert, active, intelligent little dogs. They are relatively easy to train, thriving on the discipline of organized training classes. Many Poms take part in Obedience events, loving every minute of it. Basic training should start immediately when you get your puppy, and you should enroll in organized classes as soon as your puppy is eligible.

VACCINATIONS

Vaccinations, or inoculations (throughout this chapter, the terms will be used synonymously), stimulate the dog to produce active immunity against one or more diseases, without developing any symptoms of that disease. In order to achieve this, the causative micro-organisms (bacteria or viruses) have to be altered so that they are incapable of causing the disease but can still stimulate immunity. They are therefore either killed (inactivated) or modified live (attenuated).

Once so altered, the appropriate micro-organisms can be introduced into the body by various routes. For example, the vaccination against kennel cough (infectious bronchotracheitis) is administered by nasal drops. Inoculation, on the other hand, usually involves an injection.

Regardless of whether the vaccine is inactivated or attenuated, the body produces an active immunity against it. This lasts a variable time, depending on the vaccine and the disease.

Immunity gap

Puppies are usually born with some immunity that is acquired from their mother while still in the womb. The necessary antibodies are carried in the blood and cross the placenta into the puppy. This is acquired (passive) immunity. It only lasts for about three weeks, but puppies are fortified via antibodies absorbed from the milk when suckling.

Passive protection starts to wane once weaning begins, and disappears about three to four weeks after the puppy has left the dam. This is usually the time to start vaccinations, but it is also the danger period for the puppy, since, at this time, he is susceptible to any naturally

Puppies acquire natural immunity from their mother, but it only lasts about three weeks.

acquired infection. This is the reason why you are asked to isolate your puppy until 10 to 14 days after his vaccinations while the puppy develops some immunity. During this period, the puppy is not protected.

One of the main aims of vaccine manufacturers is to develop vaccines that will confer solid protection in the shortest possible time, even when circulating maternal antibodies are present. The course of initial puppy vaccines can be completed by 10 to 12 weeks of age, affording your Pom puppy early immunity. This allows much earlier socialization and training. Subsequent boosters will be needed to maintain protection.

Once you have acquired your puppy and have allowed a day or two for him to settle in, call your veterinary clinic and inquire about vaccinations, costs, appointment details, and facilities (see page 24).

Be sure also to ask about puppy socialization classes – they are good fun and particularly useful for active, intelligent, "into everything" Pom puppies. They allow controlled interaction between puppies of all ages and breeds. Your new puppy will then get used to the fact that most of his classmates are bigger than him – something he will have to learn to live with for the rest of his life.

Vaccinations do not give lifelong immunity, and booster shots will be necessary. Recent work shows that the amount of immunity conferred varies with the disease and also whether the vaccine is attenuated or inactivated. Generally, killed vaccines confer shorter-lasting immunity and more frequent boosters are required.

Modern canine vaccines cover several diseases, sometimes offered in vaccine combinations. Some components, however, particularly the inactivated components (e.g., against leptospirosis, a bacterial disease that attacks the liver and kidneys), are known to confer only a short immunity, often measured in months.

With any combination vaccine, the efficacy of the product as a whole is considered in relation to the component that gives the shortest protection. Therefore, although protection against diseases such as distemper and hepatitis will last for much longer than a year, because these are combined with leptospirosis, the manufacturers' recommendation will be that an annual booster of the combined vaccine is advised.

Vaccine reactions

Recent concern regarding the possibility of some dogs developing reactions to booster vaccines has led manufacturers and veterinarians to begin changing their recommendations.

Vaccination programs are now tailored to the individual dog or puppy and the location in which you live. Discuss this with your veterinarian when your puppy gets his first shots.

There is concern that, in some cases, vaccinations (particularly booster shots) can overload the immune system and result in problems such as a type of anemia known as auto-immune hemolytic anaemia.

I think this risk exists, but it is a considerably smaller risk than that of the reemergence of these killer diseases if we allow our pets' immune status to fall dangerously. What can be done?

Laboratory testing of blood samples will accurately indicate whether immunity has fallen to a level where the dog is at risk, and thus a booster is advisable. However, the cost of testing for one disease will probably be equal to, if not more than, the cost of a combined revaccination for all the diseases.

Economics apart, there is also the question of stress for the dog. Taking blood samples, although relatively painless, is likely to be resented far more by your pert Pom than a simple shot to reinforce immunity against all the diseases.

Because of the concerns expressed regarding vaccination, the number of components combined in each vaccine, and the recommendation of annual boosters, vaccines have recently been arbitrarily divided into two groups: core and non-core.

Discuss any concerns you may have at the time of primary vaccination.

Core and Non-core vaccines

These are the necessary ones that protect against diseases that are serious, fatal, or difficult to treat.

In Britain, these include distemper, parvovirus and hepatitis (adenovirus). In North America, rabies is another core vaccine (this also applies to the U.K. if you intend to travel to any of the countries in the PETS scheme, which allows entry into the U.K. without having to undergo the mandatory six months' quarantine). On both sides of the Atlantic, veterinarians are unanimous in advising protection with the core vaccines.

In Britain and North America, non-core vaccines include bordetella (kennel cough) and leptospirosis. In the U.S., coronovirus and borellia (Lyme disease), which causes an infective polyarthritis, are added. This latter vaccine is known to cause reactions, and so is used only when considered essential in the U.S.

Therefore, the decision on which non-core vaccines are used depends upon risk assessment for your animal and your circumstances. This should be discussed with your vet.

For example, bordetella vaccine against kennel cough, which, in the U.K., involves the administration of nasal drops, only gives approximately six to nine months of immunity. It is valuable if your Pomeranian is going into boarding kennels or attending classes, but may not otherwise be considered necessary. Discuss these and any other problems with your vet during those all-important primary inoculation visits.

Primary inoculation is considered to be sound, preventative medicine, as is the first annual booster when the pup is about 15 months of age. Future vaccinations will depend upon the advice of your vet. Many factors influence this, including local infection levels, breed susceptibilities, and so on.

Canine distemper

Canine distemper is no longer widespread in most developed Western countries, solely due to vaccination.

Signs include fever, diarrhea, and coughing, with discharges from the nose and eyes. With the hardpad variant, the pads of the feet can harden. A significant proportion of infected dogs develop neurological signs, including fits, chorea (twitching of muscle groups), and paralysis.

Due to widespread vaccination, distemper is rare today, but this leads to a false sense of security – the virus is still out there, awaiting its opportunity. This was demonstrated in Finland only a few years ago, when a serious epidemic of distemper occurred, solely due to falling levels of immunity in the canine population.

Hepatitis

This is also known as canine adenovirus. Signs range from sudden death in peracute infection, to mild cases where the dog only appears to be a bit under the weather. In severe cases, there is usually fever, enlargement of all the lymph nodes, and a swollen liver. During recovery, blue eye can occur. This is due to the swelling of the cornea (the clear part of the front of the eye), and the dog looks blind. Although initially very worrying, this usually resolves quickly without problems.

Parvovirus

This is caused by a virus that is particularly stable – in other words, the causative virus can exist in the environment for a long time. The disease reached epidemic proportions in Europe and North America in the 1980s. Main signs include vomiting and blood-stained diarrhea. The rapid development of safe, effective vaccines brought the disease under control in the Western world, although it is still a serious killer, rivaling only distemper, in many other countries.

Rabies

Rabies is a fatal infection that affects dogs in many parts of the world, and which is easily communicated to humans. The virus is spread by bites from infected animals – which can be any warm-blooded creature (e.g., foxes, bats, stray dogs).

Signs include difficulty in swallowing; dull, staring eyes; an aversion to bright lights; drooling; and paralyzed jaws. Character changes also occur – an aggressive or wild dog may become affectionate, and a loving pet may turn into a fierce beast. There is no cure, and the animal will eventually fall into a coma. Most die within two weeks of the first symptoms.

Rabies vaccination is compulsory in many countries, including the United States, and in Britain for dogs travelling under the PETS scheme.

If you suspect your dog has rabies, you must confine him to a safe place, avoid contact with him, and immediately contact your veterinarian – who will advise you of your next step. Of course, it should never get to this stage – your dog's vaccinations should always be kept up to date.

Rabies vaccination is compulsory in many countries.

Parainfluenza

This virus is considered to be one of the primary causes of the kennel cough syndrome (infectious bronchotracheitis) in North America. *Bordetella bronchiseptica,* a bacterium, is another main cause.

A component against parainfluenza has been incorporated in multivalent vaccines for some years. The manufacturers recommend annual revaccination against parainfluenza, with the suggestion that, if your dog is going into a high-risk situation (boarding kennels, shows, etc.), even more frequent revaccination should be considered.

Kennel cough, whether due to parainfluenza virus or bacterial bordetella, is not usually life-threatening except in very young and very old dogs. Either can cause a persistent cough, and infection lasts longer than the symptoms. This carrier state results in rapid spread of the disease.

Bordetellosis

Kennel cough syndrome, infectious tracheitis, infectious bronchotracheitis – a variety of names for a disease that can spread very quickly when animals are closely congregated. Even the cause is in dispute, depending upon which side of the Atlantic you live on.

Coughing Poms are a pathetic sight. They can cough persistently for up to three weeks but seldom seem to be particularly ill. However, recent work has shown that there are very virulent strains of *Bordetella* that cause serious disease with the onset of rapid bronchopneumonia.

Unlike parainfluenza, bordetella is not incorporated into the usual multivalent vaccines. It is usually administered separately via nasal drops. These have been shown to give better immunity than conventional inoculation.

In Britain, there is a combined parainfluenza and *Bordetella* intranasal vaccine available.

Leptospirosis

The leptospira organisms that cause leptospirosis are bacterial and not viral in origin. Two forms (serovars) are combined into leptospira vaccines. *Leptospira canicola* is mainly spread in the urine of infected dogs. *Leptospira icterohaemorrhagia*, the other serovar, is spread by wild animals.

L. icterohaemorrhagia is zoonotic (communicable to humans), and this is one of

Vaccination against kennel cough will be needed if you plan to board your Pom.

the reasons that vaccination is recommended. Since it is a killed vaccine, it is probably the shortest-acting of all the various components in multivalent vaccines. Since manufacturers' recommendations regarding revaccination are based upon the shortest-acting component, there is doubt whether its inclusion is realistic. Your veterinarian will discuss this with you.

Canine coronavirus

This virus can cause diarrhea, particularly in puppies. The disease is usually mild and responds to supportive therapy.

A vaccine is available in North America and some European countries, but no licensed vaccine is currently available in Britain.

Lyme disease (borreliosis)

This bacterial disease is carried by certain ticks whose bite can transmit the disease to dogs and people. It is very common in parts of North America, and it does occur in the U.K. It causes acute joint pain in both dogs and people. Fever, heart, kidney, and neurological problems can also occur.

Although vaccines are available in North America, their use is controversial, and there is currently no licensed vaccine available in Britain.

PARASITES

Parasite control is an important part of preventative health care and is essential for all dogs, regardless of size or lifestyle. Parasites are roughly divided into two groups:

- **Ectoparasites** live on the surface of the host and include fleas, lice, ticks, and mites.
- **Endoparasites** live within the host. Worms are the most well known, but there are also other important endoparasites, such as coccidia and giardia, although these may not be quite so widespread.

Fleas

Fleas are the most common ectoparasites found on dogs. They are found worldwide, and Pomeranians, with their abundant undercoat and long guard hairs, pick them up from the environment or from contact with other animals. The thick coat provides an ideal refuge for the fleas.

Some dogs will carry a very high flea burden without problem, whereas others will show evidence of typical flea allergy dermatitis (FAD) although no fleas can be found. This is due to the development of a hypersensitivity to flea saliva as a result of being bitten.

FAD is not common in the Pomeranian, although it can occur, causing serious pruritis (itching) with considerable hair loss. In my experience, it arises as the direct result of carrying a very high, undetected flea burden. Therefore, be thorough when brushing and combing, and ensure that you part the coat and groom the full thickness of the coat, taking note of any flea dirts present on the surface of the skin. This is not easy in any full-coated dog, and particularly so in the Pomeranian.

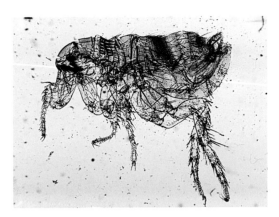

Tho dog flea – Clenooophalides canis.

Fleas are not host-specific, and infestation of many Pomeranians can be traced to the family cat. All types of fleas can bite us as well as a range of other animals.

Life cycle

Effective control involves both adult fleas on the dog and also the immature stages that develop in the home. Fleas need a meal of blood to complete their life cycle. The adult flea then lays eggs on the dog, which soon drop to the ground. Provided temperature and humidity are within the correct range, they develop into larvae (immature forms) in the carpets or gaps between floorboards.

Development can also take place outdoors, provided conditions are suitable. Many pet dogs (and cats) have various areas in the yard where they like to lie, and such areas can be difficult to render flea-free!

Under ideal conditions, the life cycle can be completed in as short a time as three weeks. Sometimes, fleas can live without feeding for more than a year, which is why dogs and people can be bitten when entering a property that has been left unoccupied for some time.

Flea control

There are many effective preparations to control adult fleas on the dog. Prolonged-action spot-on preparations are probably the most effective in the case of full-coated breeds such as the Pomeranian. They contain a chemical that is lethal to the flea. This is dissolved in a vehicle that spreads through the fat layer on the skin. Within 24 hours, the dog will have total protection against fleas for up to two months. When the flea bites your Pom, it has to penetrate the fat layer to get to the blood supply, and, by so doing, ingests the chemical.

If the dog gets wet or is bathed once or more, the efficacy of the treatment is not affected. However, it is important to reapply the preparation according to the manufacturers' recommendation, usually every 30 or 60 days, depending on the active ingredient, to ensure complete protection.

Some preparations are also effective against certain endoparasites, particularly roundworms.

Sprays can be used, but Poms usually dislike the noise, and careful parting of the thick coat is necessary to ensure that the spray application is effective.

Oral preparations are also available, which prevent the completion of the flea's life cycle. The compound is transferred to the adult flea when it bites the dog for the all-essential blood meal.

Insecticidal baths are useful for killing adult fleas in the coat, but they do not have a lasting effect. I would not advise bathing as a first line of treatment for fleas on your Pomeranian. Bathing should always be combined with other methods of flea control to reduce rapid reinfestation.

Adult fleas account for only approximately 5 percent of the total flea population. Control of the other 95 percent, consisting of immature stages, can be much more difficult. Few environmental insecticides have any effect against immature fleas, so an insecticide with prolonged action should be used. This will be effective against any subsequently emerging adults.

Control in the home should also involve thorough vacuuming to remove any flea larvae.

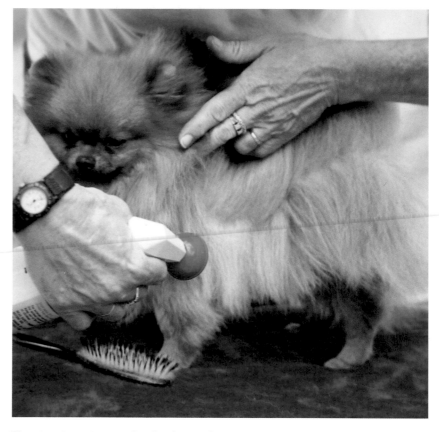

Flea treatment can take the form of a spray.

Lice

It is only infrequently that I have encountered lice on Pomeranians, and these have, without exception, been on puppy mill animals.

Lice require direct contact for transmission, and, unlike fleas, the whole life cycle occurs on the host. The eggs (nits) are attached to individual hairs. Infestation is usually associated with violent itching and often affects the head and ears.

Unlike fleas, lice can be controlled by bathing in an effective ectoparasite shampoo.

Ticks

Ticks are carriers of various diseases, including Lyme disease (*borelliosis*), babesiosis, and ehrlichiosis. Although these diseases have been recognized in the U.K., they are more common in warmer parts of Europe and the United States.

Poms that are exercised in the country are more likely to pick up ticks and mites.

Several flea and lice preparations are effective for tick control. Your veterinarian will advise you on the best choice.

Cheyletiellosis

Cheyletiella yasguri, a type of mite, can just be seen by the naked eye as a tiny white speck, hence the term "walking dandruff." The condition is not uncommon in young Poms acquired from large kennels. Young animals appear to have dandruff and be itchy.

The mite is zoonotic and can cause intense irritation, particularly in children. Adult dogs who are themselves symptomless spread cheyletiella in kennels.

Sprays, bathing, and spot-on preparations are all effective, but other pets should be treated to ensure that reinfestation does not recur. Veterinary advice is important.

Ear mites

The *otodectes cynotis* mite is red in color and just visible to the naked eye. They can be picked up by dogs exercised in fields and woodlands. These mites primarily infest a dog's ears, but other parts of the head may be affected.

Because the dog's ears are involved, special medication is necessary. It's important to see your veterinarian if your dog is scratching his ears or holding his head to one side. You may also see a dark, granular substance in the ears.

Ear mites are not that common in Pomeranians.

Mange

Mange is a parasitic skin disease caused by microscopic mites. Two types of mite cause mange in dogs: **demodectic** and **sarcoptic** mites. Neither, in my experience, are a particular problem in the Pomeranian, but both demodectic and sarcoptic mange occur in the breed occasionally.

Demodectic mange

Demodex mites live in the hair follicles and sebaceous glands of many normal dogs. They only cause problems if the host becomes immunocompromised for any reason. It is for this reason that demodectic mange is not thought of as a contagious disease in the same way as sarcoptic mange.

If the demodex mite starts to multiply, signs including inflammation and hair loss are seen. Often, itching is minimal, but secondary bacterial infection can be a problem.

Veterinary treatment using modern preparations is effective once a positive diagnosis has been made.

Sarcoptic mange

Sarcoptic mange is zoonotic. It is also intensely pruritic (itchy). Children are particularly susceptible. It causes scabies, and itchy areas develop on the arms and abdomen when an affected animal is cared for.

A program of preventative worming should be followed throughout your Pom's life.

Modern veterinary treatments are effective but depend on accurate diagnosis, which sometimes requires repeated skin scrapings. Consult your veterinarian if you are concerned.

Endoparasites

Intestinal worms are by far the most important endoparasites in the dog. Protozoan parasites, such as coccidia and giardia, may also be a problem in certain areas, particularly in North America.

Roundworms (nematodes)

Until relatively recently, all puppies were considered to have worms. An understanding of the complex life cycle, together with the development of more effective roundworm remedies, have resulted in a dramatic reduction in the number of worm-infested dogs and puppies.

The most common roundworm is *Toxacara canis*. This is a large, round, white worm 3 to 6 inches (7–15 cm) long. The life cycle is complex. Puppies can be born with toxocariasis acquired from their mother before birth. Regular worming of puppies and adults is essential. It is worthwhile remembering that the worm is the same size no matter whether it infests the bowel of a Great Dane or your tiny Pomeranian.

Roundworm larvae can remain dormant in the tissues of adult dogs indefinitely. In the bitch, under the influence of hormones during pregnancy, they become activated, cross the placenta, and enter the puppy, where they finally develop into adult worms in the small intestine. Larvae can also be passed from the bitch to the puppy during suckling.

There are now many safe and effective worm treatments available. Endecticides are spot-on preparations. They are similar to those used for flea control, but contain drugs such as selamectin that will be effective not only against fleas but also against roundworms and heartworms.

Preparations are available today that are licensed for use in puppies – even tiny Pomeranian puppies – from 14 days of age. Many preparations are available over the counter, but veterinary advice is worthwhile to establish an effective lifelong worming strategy.

There is a slight risk of roundworms being transmitted to humans. For this reason, veterinarians advise that all adult dogs be routinely wormed approximately twice a year.

Tapeworms (cestodes)

This is the other common type of intestinal worm found in the dog. Unlike roundworms, they do not have a direct life cycle, so spread is not from dog to dog but through an intermediate host. This varies according to the type of tapeworm. Intermediate hosts include fleas, sheep, horses, rodents, and sometimes humans.

In the dog, the most common type of tapeworm is *Dipylidium caninum*. This worm, which can be up to 20 inches (50 cm) long, uses the flea as the intermediate host. The worms live in the intestine. Eggs contained within mature segments are shed from the end of the worm and pass out in the dog's feces. These segments are sticky and look like small grains of rice. They can often be seen attached to hairs around the anus in infested dogs. The segments finally drop to the ground, dry, and burst, releasing the microscopic eggs.

The Pom is a lively dog, and accidents can happen all too easily.

hosts include rabbits, hares, and similar wildlife that they catch and eat.

Tapeworms of *Echinococcus* species deserve mention, since they are important in dogs in general because of their zoonotic potential. Dogs are generally infected by eating infected raw meat, thus the risk for your Pomeranian is relatively small.

Echinococcus multilocularis is a tapeworm that can cause serious cysts in the lungs of people. Not indigenous in Britain, it can be found in many other parts of the world. Dogs entering Britain under the PETS scheme have to be treated with specific remedies against this cestode and must be so certified before entry or re-entry is allowed. This should be borne in mind if you intend to travel to any of the PETS authorized countries from Britain with your Pomeranian. Ask your veterinarian for more details.

Free-living flea larvae eat these eggs, which develop as the flea matures. When the adult flea is swallowed by a susceptible dog, the life cycle of the tapeworm is completed.

Effective eradication involves vigorous flea control, including the developing flea larvae in the environment. Therefore, although tapeworm remedies can be bought over the counter, it is a wise strategy to seek veterinary help.

Other tapeworms cause problems in dogs, but these are more common in larger dogs with an outdoor lifestyle since the intermediate

Heartworm

Heartworm (*Dirofilaria immitis*) causes major problems in many of the warmer parts of the world, including North America. Selamectin, mentioned previously, is one of the effective drugs available. Consult your veterinarian if heartworm is a problem in your area.

Other intestinal worms

Hookworms (uncinaria and ancylostoma species), together with whipworms (*Trichuris vulpis*), are occasionally the cause of lack of condition. More severe signs, such as anemia or dysentery, can occur. These worms are usually associated with kenneled dogs. They are often discovered during routine fecal investigation rather than because of illness.

Treatment is uncomplicated with modern dewormers prescribed by your vet.

A Pom owner should be aware of the principles of first aid.

Giardia and Coccidia

These microscopic protozoan endoparasites can cause diarrhea problems, particularly in puppies. Giardia is a waterborne disease, more common in North America than in Britain.

Giardiasis is considered to be zoonotic and is the most common intestinal parasite in humans in America. Nevertheless, there is no conclusive evidence that cysts shed by dogs (and cats) are infective to humans. If you are concerned, a simple stool test can be carried out by your veterinarian.

EMERGENCY CARE AND FIRST AID

Pomeranians are pert, active little dogs with a thick coat, but all sorts of emergencies can occur. Bites, burns, broken legs, heat stroke, insect stings, and poisoning are just a few. All occur without warning – otherwise they would not be emergencies!

First aid is the initial treatment given in any emergency. The purpose is to preserve life, reduce pain and discomfort, minimize the risk of permanent disability or disfigurement, and prevent further injury.

Emergency procedures

Regardless of the cause, in any emergency there is a certain protocol that it is worthwhile to observe.

- Keep calm and do not panic.
- Get help if possible.
- Contact your veterinarian, explain the situation, and obtain advice specific for the problem.

- If there is possible internal injury, try to keep the patient as still as possible. With a dog the size of a Pomeranian, placing him in a cardboard box or other makeshift container is a good idea, but make sure that he cannot injure himself further by jumping out. Use the box to transport your pet to the veterinarian as soon as possible.
- Drive carefully and observe the speed limits.

Depending on the nature of the emergency, it may be necessary to carry out first aid on site. Following a sequential routine is the most efficient approach. Therefore, follow the A, B, C of first aid:

A is for Airway

This means checking the mouth and throat, and ensuring that there is no obstruction preventing air from reaching the lungs.

B is for Breathing

Check to see if there are signs of breathing.

C is for Circulation

Make sure the heart is beating.

How does this work? Imagine a dog choking because there is something lodged in his mouth or throat. **A** is for **Airway:** You first try to remove any blockage before doing anything else. Take care! Remember that the most docile, affectionate pet in such a situation will be terrified. Try to avoid using your fingers, as you might get badly bitten. Use a stick or other blunt implement to gently dislodge anything in the mouth. Wrap tissues around the instrument in order to remove any vomit, saliva, etc.

Once the airway is clear, go to **B**, check for **Breathing**. Place the palm of your hand around the chest, just behind the forelegs. Can you feel a heartbeat (**C** for **Circulation**), and is the chest moving? If there is no movement of the ribs and you can feel no heartbeat (pulse), artificial respiration and cardiac massage can be easily combined in a dog the size of a Pomeranian.

Canine CPR

The heart is situated in the lower part of the chest, just at the level of the elbows. With your hand around the sternum, fingers one side and the thumb the other, start gently squeezing approximately 20 to 25 times a minute. This has the dual function of stimulating the heart and helping to get air into the lungs. About every ten squeezes or so, check for a heartbeat or any breathing. If you manage to start the heart, continue for several minutes. This is **cardiopulmonary resuscitation** (CPR).

Check the color of the mucous membranes of the gums or under the lips. When you first started, they were probably white or ashen gray. Once the heart is beating, a vague pink tinge should return. This return to color will be very subtle, because your dog will likely be in shock.

Shock tactics

Shock is a complex condition disrupting the delicate fluid balance of the body. It is always accompanied by a serious fall in blood pressure. Causes include serious hemorrhage, heart failure, heatstroke, and acute allergic reactions (e.g., bee stings).

Signs of shock can include:

- Rapid breathing,
- Rapid heart rate,
- Pallor of the mucous membranes of the gums, lips, and under the eyelids,
- Severe depression,
- A cold feel to the limbs, ears, etc.,
- Sometimes vomiting.

The most important first-aid treatment for shock is to keep the dog warm. Do not apply too much external heat – instead, wrap him in blankets, newspapers, clothes, whatever is available, and get him to your vet as soon as possible.

In the rest of this section, I am going to outline a brief first-aid procedure for some of the common emergencies that can occur with your Pomeranian. The list is by no means comprehensive, but knowledge of the correct approach for treating these conditions should help you if you are confronted with any emergency.

Bleeding

In Pomeranians, quite severe bleeding can occur from torn nails, which, if overgrown, can catch in floor coverings. Torn nails and cuts on the pads and limbs should be bandaged fairly tightly using a clean bandage or any clean material. A plastic bag can then be bandaged onto the limb to prevent further blood loss.

Bleeding from other parts of the body, including the head, ears, etc., cannot be so easily controlled. In these cases, try applying a cold-water swab and finger or hand pressure.

Burns

Although their thick coats can be protective, burns do occur in Pomeranians. Frequently, examination immediately after the event shows no abnormality. Nevertheless, cool the burned area with cold water as quickly as possible. If it is due to a caustic substance, such as drain cleaner or bleach, wash away as much as you can with plenty of cold water.

Even if there does not seem too much cause for concern, get your dog to your veterinarian as soon as you can. This will often avoid the peeling skin that can develop on a burned area a few days later.

Eye injuries

Although Pomeranians do not have very prominent eyes, nevertheless they are vulnerable. Scratches from bushes, cats' claws, and grass seeds are common injuries. Cold water, or better still, saline solution (contact lens solution), liberally applied with a pad, should be used to cleanse the eye. If the eyeball appears to be injured or if there is any bleeding, try to cover with a cold-water-soaked pad and get to your veterinarian as soon as possible.

The Pom's eyes can be vulnerable to injury.

Heatstroke

In warm, humid weather, heatstroke can occur rapidly. Hot houses and poorly ventilated rooms can be just as dangerous as cars. The dog does not have to be in the sun for heatstroke to strike.

- First signs are excessive panting with obvious distress. Coma and death can quickly follow, due to irreversible changes in the blood vessels.
- Reduce the temperature as quickly as possible, plunging or bathing the animal in cold water.
- Place ice on the gums, under the tail, and in the groin.
- Then take the still-wet animal to the veterinarian as soon as possible.

Seizures

During a seizure, your dog is unconscious and does not know what is happening. It is pretty terrifying for any onlookers.

It is important to prevent injury while the dog is thrashing about. A cardboard box is useful. Immediately after the seizure, the dog is unlikely to be able to see, hear, or feel properly, and therefore will be less likely to frighten or injure himself if suitably confined. Subdued light will hasten the dog's recovery.

Most seizures only last a few seconds or minutes, although it may seem very much longer to you. If your Pom is still seizuring after five minutes or so, telephone your veterinarian for advice. Otherwise, once he has come out of the seizure and is fairly conscious, take him to your veterinarian – still in the container, if possible.

BREED-SPECIFIC PROBLEMS

Many members of the Toy group do suffer breed-specific conditions, but the Pomeranian has few genuine breed-specific problems. For example, dental problems are widely recognized in Toy breeds, yet Pomeranians are less affected than many of their small-breed canine cousins.

Luxating patella

A normal kneecap moves in a groove at the lower end of the femur (thigh bone). Some dogs are born with a groove that is not deep enough to retain the kneecap so that it will pop out of the groove, usually to the inside of the joint. This is called luxating patella, or slipping kneecap. It causes the dog to hop for a few steps.

If mildly affected, the kneecap will often return to its groove and the signs will disappear. Sometimes both legs are affected, and, particularly if the Pomeranian is overweight, the condition can be crippling.

Often it first becomes noticeable when a puppy is as young as five to ten months, when, occasionally, the puppy may appear to hop on one of his hind legs.

Today, there are very successful surgical techniques available to correct the problem. It is wise to refrain from breeding from any affected individuals.

Cryptorchidism

In male Pom puppies, both testes (testicles) should be present in the scrotum at the time of purchase.

However, occasionally they do not descend from the abdomen on cue. If they have not descended by the time the dog is adult, he is described as either unilaterally cryptorchid (one testis retained) or bilaterally cryptorchid (when both are undescended and are retained in the abdomen).

It is worthwhile checking with your veterinarian at the time of your first check-up whether or not both testes are where they should be in the scrotum.

Breed-specific problems are relatively rare among Poms.

Dental problems

Like many tiny dogs, Pomeranians do suffer dental problems at an earlier age than you would expect. Periodontitis affects many Toy breeds.

In the Pomeranian, much can be done to reduce the problem if regular home care procedures are adopted from an early age.

There are many special chews, foods, toys, etc. available to delay dental problems, and regular

With good care and management, your Pom should live a long, happy, healthy life.

brushing with a suitable canine toothbrush and paste is worthwhile.

The earlier the home care regimen is put into place, the easier your pet accepts it as part of his regular routine (see Chapter Five).

SUMMARY

Although tiny in size, the Pom is a healthy dog, with the robustness of his large, spitz-type cousins. His larger-than-life character also belies his size. Cheerful and affectionate, he is simply a joy to live with and makes for a loving, faithful companion.